D1029500

LETTERS OF WARREN AKIN
CONFEDERATE CONGRESSMAN

WARREN AKIN
1811-1877

MARY VERDERY AKIN
1830-1907

Letters of Warren Akin
Confederate Congressman

Edited By

BELL IRVIN WILEY
PROFESSOR OF HISTORY
EMORY UNIVERSITY

☆ ☆ ☆
☆ ☆
☆

UNIVERSITY OF GEORGIA PRESS
ATHENS

Library of Congress Catalog Card No. 59-15538
Printed in the United States of America

☆ ☆ ☆

Contents

☆ ☆ ☆

Introduction

THE Congress that represented the Southern people during their unsuccessful bid for independence in 1861-1865 is one of the least known subjects in Confederate history.[1] Several circumstances are responsible for the relative obscurity of this branch of the Confederate Government.

In the first place, many of the deliberations were secret. When the legislators voted to go into secret session, as they frequently did before considering important bills, newspaper reporters were barred from the halls and no record was kept of the debates.

A second reason for the paucity of information about doings of Congress is the skimpiness of its records. Clerks kept a journal of proceedings, consisting of a record of acts considered and their disposition, but even this meagre account was not published until many years after the war.[2] About the only source of information concerning Congressional activities available to the people of the time were the session statutes published by official act of Congress (and these did not include certain secret laws), occasional committee reports, various acts and resolutions printed as separates for limited circulation, and proceedings of non-secret sessions published in the newspapers.[3]

A third explanation for dearth of information about the Confederate Congress is to be found in faulty public relations. News-

---

1. An unpublished doctoral dissertation at the University of North Carolina (1949), by W. B. Yearns, is devoted to the Confederate Congress. Its emphasis is on legislation rather than on personnel. The best published account of the Congress and its work is in E. M. Coulter, *The Confederate States of America, 1861-1865* (Baton Rouge, 1950), 134-48.

2. *Journal of the Congress of the Confederate States* (7 vols. Washington, 1904-1905).

3. James M. Matthews, ed., *Statutes at Large of the Confederate States of America* (Richmond, 1862-1864) and James M. Matthews, ed., *Statutes at Large of the Provisional Government of the Confederate States of America* (Richmond, 1864). Matthews' compilations did not include the acts of

papers, and the public in general, came to resent greatly the secrecy in which Congress enshrouded its activities. Offense created by closed sessions often developed into antipathy toward the Congress. Moreover, ignorance of what the legislators actually were doing led to suspicion of their motives and actions, and gave rise to all sorts of rumors, some of which were fantastic in the extreme. Throughout most of its career, Congress had what is known today as a poor press. Newspapermen, irritated by their inability to get first-hand information about legislative activities, seemed to derive great pleasure in berating Congressmen individually and collectively, and in playing up the eccentricities and shortcomings of some of the least capable and most sensational members.

Unquestionably the Confederate Congress had its shortcomings. It devoted far too much time to long-winded discussion of trivialities. It sometimes showed ignorance of prior legislation, and was by no means consistent in its actions. Some of its members were loud-mouthed demagogues, lamentably deficient in character and statesmanship. Others were run-of-the-mill politicians whose chief interest was in keeping their positions and drawing their pay. But some were men of outstanding ability, and a majority appeared to have been conscientious, honorable persons who rendered creditable service to the country and their constituents.

Certainly the Confederate Congress was not the incompetent, inefficient, spineless, debating society that its critics alleged it to be. And, on the whole, it deserves a higher rating than historians have accorded it. It had the foresight and boldness to enact the first national conscription act in American history. Its tax-in-kind and impressment laws were imaginative, far-reaching measures which represented radical departures from precedent. A

---

the second session of the Second Congress. These, along with secret acts of previous sessions, were compiled by Charles W. Ramsdell from scattered sources and published in 1941 by the Duke University Press. In his introduction and bibliographical note, Professor Ramsdell gives valuable information about the registering and publication of the statutes and the various titles and editions of their publication. See Chas. W. Ramsdell, ed., *Laws and Joint Resolutions of the Last Session of the Confederate Congress (November 7, 1864-March 1865) Together with the Secret Acts of Previous Congresses* (Durham, 1941), ix-xxiii.

considerable number of Congressmen who voted for conscription, impressment, and suspension of the writ of habeas corpus were personally opposed to these acts, but they gave their assent because the President and the leading military authorities held that these laws were essential to the public interest.

A fourth reason for lack of information about the Confederate Congress is the scarcity of personal documents bearing on the composition and work of that body. Apparently very, very few of the Rebel lawmakers kept diaries during their Congressional terms. They wrote many letters, but save for routine and unrevealing communications of an unofficial nature, only a small portion of these are now known to be extant. For several years the writer has been conducting a diligent search for personal letters and diaries written by Confederate Congressmen during their terms of office. The results, while yielding a few substantial collections, have been disappointingly meagre. For many Congressmen not one personal letter has been found. This circumstance makes especially gratifying the discovery of the Warren Akin letters here reproduced.

* * * * *

Three Congresses sat during the period of the Confederacy.[4] A unicameral body known as the Provisional Congress held five sessions, the first of which convened at Montgomery, Alabama, on February 4, 1861, and the last of which adjourned at Richmond—to which the government was transferred in May, 1861—on February 17, 1862. The members of the Provisional Congress were chosen by the secession conventions rather than by popular vote. The primary mission of the Provisional Congressmen was the organization of the new government and the adoption of a constitution. But they early assumed legislative functions and acted as the national lawmaking body until their final adjournment.

4. For detailed information about the sessions of Congress, and a complete list of members, by state, see: *Executive and Congressional Directory of the Confederate States, 1861-1865* (Washington, 1899).

On February 18, 1862, a new bicameral Congress, chosen by popular vote the preceding fall, assembled in Richmond. This body, known as the First Congress, held four sessions before going out of existence on February 17, 1864. The last Congress, designated officially as the Second Congress, held two sessions extending over the period May 2, 1864-March 18, 1865.

All in all, 267 men served in the Confederate Congress, and at least one other was elected who was unable to take his seat before the Confederacy, in the jargon of the times, "went up the spout."[5] About one in three of this number had served in the Federal Congress, and most of them had obtained political experience of some kind in their own states.[6]

The life of a Confederate Congressman was for the most part unenviable. Many of the problems with which the legislators had to cope were impossible of solution in that they derived from the effort of "a nation with nothing," founded on the outmoded philosophy of state rights, to win independence in a gigantic, modern war with an established power that seemed by contrast to have everything. The ultimate result was frustration and failure; and in the long time that intervened between the hopeful beginning and final defeat most Congressmen were subjected to considerable abuse by journalists, members of other departments of the government, state authorities, constituents, and the public in general. Compensation was woefully inadequate. The pay scale at the beginning of the war was $8.00 a day with travel allowance of ten cents a mile for official trips between home and capital. Salaries were increased in 1862 to $2,760 a year and mileage to twenty cents. Further increases were voted with the result that early in 1865 Congressmen were getting $690 a month. Even so, salaries lagged so far behind soaring prices that Congressmen ex-

5. This member was Nathaniel W. Townes of Texas, chosen in a special election held on March 13, 1865, to fill a vacancy caused by the death of Simpson H. Morgan, member of the Confederate House of Representatives. Congress adjourned before he could take his seat and his name does not appear in the *Executive and Congressional Directory* published in 1899. See R. J. Townes to Governor Pendleton Murrah, May 1, 1865, MS, Texas State Archives.

6. Coulter, *Confederate States*, 134.

perienced great difficulty in sustaining themselves on their meagre stipends, much less in supporting their families at home.[7]

Some of the Congressmen stayed in hotels, and a directory published in 1864 shows that the Exchange, the Ballard House, and the Spotswood were favorite places of abode. A few legislators bought or rented houses in the capital. But the majority of them lived in boarding houses or private homes.[8] On May 25, 1864, Congressman A. M. Branch of Texas wrote his wife: "I am now paying $600 per month with two meals a day which is pretty high Board."[9] In April of the same year, Thomas A. Harris of Missouri wrote his governor: "The pay . . . does not exceed $10 or $11 per day and board alone, without washing, clothing or incidentals of any kind, is at hotels, $30 per day and at the most mediocre boarding houses from $8 to $12 per day. With my family my absolute expenses average $50 per day & you know that I live very plainly & with rigid economy."[10]

The hard-pressed Congressmen resorted to all sorts of expedients to save money. Some of them appeared to have kept bachelor establishments and to have depended largely for food and other necessities on periodic shipments from home.

Wives and families, in some instances, suffered greater hardship than their Congressional menfolk. Women who had to take over supervision of plantations and slaves during the absence of their spouses in Richmond often found their duties exceedingly onerous. On April 12, 1862, Mrs. W. W. Boyce of South Carolina wrote her husband: "Several pigs have died. . . . I tell [you] candidly all this attention to farming is up hill work with me. I can give orders first-rate, but when I am not obeyed, I can't keep my temper. A house keeper has so much to do independent of field work. Then our [soldiers' aid] society keeps us busy. I am ever ready to give you a helping hand, but I must say I am heartily tired of trying to manage *free* negroes. . . . I do hope congress will ad-

7. *Ibid.*, 139-40; Warren Akin to his wife, Dec. 29, 1864.

8. *Directory of the House of Representatives* (Richmond, 1864); *Directory of the Confederate States Senate, Second Session, Second Congress* (Richmond, 1864).

9. A. M. Branch to his wife, May 25, 1864, MS, Huntington Library.

10. Thomas A. Harris to Gov. Thomas L. Reynolds, April 2, 1864, MS, Huntington Library.

journ sooner than you think, it is so lonesome here. . . . I beg you to come home."[11]

But the lot of a plantation woman such as Mrs. Boyce, who had Negroes to raise the crops and do the chores, whose kinfolk were nearby and from whom the Yankees were far away until early 1865, was relatively easy. The families of many Congressmen became refugees fleeing from place to place before the Federal armies, seeking hospitality of relatives and neighbors. C. C. Clay, a Confederate Senator from Huntsville, Alabama, was driven from his home early in the war. From Columbus, Georgia, one of the several places he and his wife lived as refugees, he wrote a fellow Senator on August 5, 1863: "My home & parents & most of my kindred [are] in the hands of my enemy & I an exile wandering about like a troubled spirit seeking rest."[12]

* * * * *

Warren Akin's experience was similar to that of Clay, in that he and his family had to abandon their home in Cassville, Georgia, and live as exiles for more than a year.

After an unascertainable period of education in Elbert County, where he was born on October 9, 1811, and one term in a Walton County school, Akin studied law. He was admitted to the bar and moved to Bartow (then Cass) County in 1836, where he rose rapidly to eminence as an attorney.[13] From the beginning of his legal career he manifested an active interest in politics. In 1840 he was a Whig Presidential elector and in 1850 he represented

11. Mrs. W. W. Boyce to her husband, April 12, 1862, MS in private possession.

12. C. C. Clay to L. T. Wigfall, Aug. 5, 1863. Typescript, University of Texas, of original MS in Library of Congress.

13. In Lucy Cunyus, *History of Bartow County* (Cartersville, Ga., 1933), 42, Akin's entry into the legal profession is recounted thus: "A visit to an Elberton court scene decided his profession and at the age of 10 made his vow 'to be a lawyer.' . . . [Some 8 years later] While clerking in a store in Monroe, the excitement over the Dahlonega gold mines reached Warren, and with a knap-sack on his shoulder, he walked to the new Eldorado. While working there he studied law and was admitted to the bar in Cherokee superior court, March 15, 1836 and immediately moved to Cassville. . . . His first law partner was the Hon. A. R. Wright. By 1845 he had made $7,000." Akin saved two nuggets obtained in his gold mining days and later gave them to his wife. Mrs. Akin had them made into two gold rings, one for Sally May Akin and the other for Paul. Paul used his as his wedding ring. Sally May Akin to Bell I. Wiley, September 7, 1956.

Cass County in the convention that approved the Great Compromise and adopted the "Georgia Platform." In 1859 Akin was the candidate of the Opposition Party in an unsuccessful effort to win the governorship from the Democratic incumbent, Joseph E. Brown.[14]

Like many other Southerners of Whig background, Akin was opposed to secession, but when Georgia left the Union, he felt it his duty to support his state and the new national government of which it became a part. He represented his county in the legislature from 1861 to 1863, and was Speaker of the House during this period. One act for which he was in large measure responsible while Speaker and in which he took much pride was that changing the name of his county from Cass to Bartow.[15]

On May 5, 1845, Akin married Eliza Hooper, who died two years later. His second wife was Mary Frances Verdery, daughter of Augustus N. Verdery of Floyd County, Georgia, whom he married on October 12, 1848. Akin's first wife bore him a daughter. Thirteen more children were born to him after his second marriage. Four children died before or during the war and only six grew to maturity.

Manuscript census returns indicate that in June, 1860, Akin's family consisted of himself; his second wife; a daughter, Eliza H., age 13; and four sons, Elbert, Thomas Warren, Henry Clay, and John Wesley, whose respective ages were 10, 8, 3, and 1.[16] These returns also show that Akin's real property was valued at $6,150 and his personal property, which included several slaves, was valued at $61,230.

During the first years of the war Akin devoted himself mainly to his law practice in Cassville and to his duties as a state legislator in Milledgeville. He was in Richmond when the first battle of Manassas took place, but the purpose of this trip to the Confederate capital is not known.

---

14. I. W. Avery, *History of the State of Georgia from 1850 to 1881* (New York, 1881), 95-96.

15. Paul Akin to Bell I. Wiley, Aug. 29, 1956.

16. Records kept by the Akin family indicate that the ages of Thomas Warren and Henry Clay were respectively 9 and 2 in June, 1860, rather than 10 and 3 as given in the census.

The crippling defeat inflicted on Bragg's army in the Chattanooga campaign, November 23-25, 1863, convinced Akin that a Federal drive toward Atlanta was only a matter of time. So, he began preparations to take his family out of the path of invasion.[17] Late in January, 1864, the Akins moved to Oxford, Georgia, a quiet village about thirty miles southeast of Atlanta. But the sojourn in Oxford was of short duration, as the investment of Atlanta and the Stoneman raid in the summer of 1864 necessitated a hasty departure. Akin narrowly escaped capture by the raiders.

In August, 1864, the Akin family settled in Elberton, Georgia, seat of Warren Akin's native county, home of some of his relatives, and a place of refuge for many other exiles from the Cassville area.

Warren Akin had a special reason for wanting to elude the Federals. In the autumn of 1863 he was chosen by voters of the tenth district of Georgia to serve in the lower house of the Second Confederate Congress that was to assemble the following May. He was able to avoid capture by the invaders, but on their initial visit in May, 1864—six months before kindling the fires which destroyed most of the remainder of the town—they burned his law office and residence and destroyed many items of personal property that had been left behind when the family moved to Oxford.[18]

Meanwhile Akin had taken his seat in the first session of the Congress which convened in Richmond on May 2, 1864. *The Journal of the Confederate Congress* indicates that he attended meetings regularly until June 9 when he was granted a leave of absence five days before adjournment of the first session of the Second Congress. The *Journal* does not state the reason for the leave but he probably wanted to get away from the capital as

17. The departure of the Akin family from Cassville and some of their experiences in exile are interestingly narrated in Sally May Akin, "Refugees of 1863," in *Georgia Historical Quarterly*, XXX, (1947), 112-17. Miss Akin is a daughter of Warren Akin, the Congressman.

18. According to Paul F. Akin, three Cassville dwellings, all of which housed persons too ill to be moved, were spared by the invaders. The burning of Cassville is discussed in Cunyus, *History of Bartow County*, 244, and Joseph B. Mahan, "The History of Old Cassville" (M.A. Thesis, University of Georgia, 1950), 122-29.

early as possible to help his family prepare for the move to Elberton.

Akin apparently spent the summer and the first part of the autumn of 1864 with his family. An outstanding event of this period was the birth of a daughter, Susie Henry, on October 24, 1864.

Susie's arrival caused Akin to be absent when the Second Congress convened for its second session on November 7, 1864. He did not take his seat until November 28. With the exception of a day's absence on February 3, he seems to have been in regular attendance until February 27, 1865, when Congress granted him another leave. He apparently set out for home about this time, as the *Journal* records no action of his after February 22, 1865, and a letter that he wrote from Elberton on March 11 states that he arrived there on March 5 after a "long and tedious journey through the country."

The reasons for Akin's leaving Congress nearly a month before adjournment cannot be definitely stated. That his family needed him and that he longed to be with them is clearly revealed by his letters. But these letters also reveal a strong sense of duty impelling him to remain on the job in Richmond. His eldest son, Elbert, died on February 11, 1865, from a pony-riding accident suffered three days before. But this could not have influenced Akin's early departure from Richmond since news of the tragedy did not reach him until a short time before his arrival home.

The most reasonable explanation of Akin's action is that he was convinced by the early part of 1865 that the Confederacy's collapse was imminent and that his further participation in Congressional proceedings was futile.

During the eighteen weeks that he actually sat in the Confederate Congress, Akin seems to have devoted himself conscientiously to his duties and to have played an active, though not a leading, part in legislative activities. He served as a member of the House Committee on Claims and introduced some twenty-four measures, most of which were minor amendments or routine resolutions. He sponsored no major act but, in view of the brevity of his incumbency, this is not surprising.

His legislative proposals and voting record reflect credit on him as a man and public servant. He repeatedly registered opposition to secret deliberations. He sought to restrict debates to reasonable limits and favored extending the hours of meeting to hasten Congressional action on pressing questions. He indicated friendliness toward the common people by supporting moves to curb speculation and to discontinue exemption of slave-owners from military service, and by voting to increase the pay of enlisted men and to give them the right to participate with lieutenants and captains in the election of field-grade officers.

Bills which received most attention in Congress during Akin's attendance were those advocating suspension of the writ of habeas corpus, increase of taxation, and enlistment of slaves as soldiers. Akin favored all these proposals, with qualification. He wanted suspension of the writ to be authorized only by the President, the Secretary of War, or the Commanding General of the Trans-Mississippi Department and to be restricted to cases involving treason or overt disloyalty. Like most of his colleagues, he accepted reluctantly and as a last resort the policy of putting slaves into Confederate uniforms, and he insisted that those inducted should be furnished by the states on the President's requisition and not by Confederate draft. He seems to have supported a proposal to increase Confederate revenues by doubling the tax-in-kind that had been adopted in April, 1863.

Akin's record in the Confederate Congress was such as to justify labeling him an "administration man," though he did not always support the position taken by the executive branch of the government. He voted to override the Presidential veto of a bill to provide free delivery of newspapers to soldiers. But he came to Davis's defense when the move to appoint a general-in-chief for the Confederate armies was under consideration in January, 1865, by proposing an amendment to the effect that the appointment would not interfere with the President's rights and duties as Commander-in-Chief. On the same day he refused to support a resolution calling for restoration of Joseph E. Johnston to command of the Army of Tennessee; since his home letters indicate that he wanted Johnston to have this position, it is reasonable to assume that his negative vote was based on a conviction that the resolution was an infringement on the President's constitutional prerogative.

Akin's support of the administration may have been influenced by his high regard for Jefferson Davis. On January 9, 1865, he had a long talk with Davis. The next day, in one of the most revealing and historically important passages of his correspondence, he wrote his wife the following impression of the Chief Executive:

> He has been greatly wronged. He does not control the generals in the field. He did not send Hood to Tenn. He has been trying to get Genl Lee to accept the command of all our armies, but he declined. The President is not the stern, puffed up man he is represented to be. He was as polite, attentive and communicative to me as I could wish. He listened patiently to all I said and when he differed with me he would give his reasons for it. He was very cordial in his reception of me, and in his invitation to me to call again. And many gentlemen tell me the same thing as to his manner with them. His enemies have done him a great injustice. He is a patriot and a good man, I think. He will have to do something more than anything he has done before I can denounce him. He is the best man in the Government for his place. Many want him out of office. Were he removed today we should be *ruined* in a few months, and I fear we shall any way.

Akin must have seen Davis on one of the President's better days; or else, the President, who was under severe attack in Congress at the time, consciously turned on in full force the charm that he was so capable of commanding. That Akin's confidence in the Chief Executive was not shared by a majority of his colleagues is evidenced by the fact that the Georgian's amendment, introduced a few days later, stating that the appointment of a general-in-chief should not interfere with the President's authority as Commander-in-Chief was rejected by a vote of 51 to 24.[19]

Akin occasionally criticized his fellow legislators for their slowness and long-windedness. His severest comment was the statement made to his wife on January 30, 1865: "I . . . feel like we are doing nothing as we ought. Congress seems not to realize the magni-

19. *Journal of Confed. Cong.*, VII, 462.

tude of the duties devolved upon it." But he must have been fully aware of the fact that democratic processes were by their very nature subject to periods of halting and fumbling, that deliberative bodies were often not as bungling as they seemed, and that some of the difficulties with which he and his colleagues had to deal were insurmountable. These considerations probably tended to make him restrained in his judgments and tolerant in his outlook.

With one exception he seems to have gotten along well with his Congressional colleagues. The exception was the erratic, bumptious, verbose and vitriolic Henry S. Foote of Tennessee whom Professor E. Merton Coulter has aptly dubbed "the prince of Congressional villains."[20] Foote's seat was next to Akin's, a fact which probably worked against their cordiality, as the Tennessean must have given caustic expression to his extreme hatred of President Davis. When Foote took leave of Richmond in December, 1864, after saying that he never intended to resume his place in Congress, Akin wrote to his wife: "Most of the members will be glad. . . . When he left he gave his seat to Mr. H. W. Bruce of Ky. who is a nice man, and I am delighted with the change."[21]

But Foote did return, after being arrested by Confederate military authorities as he was trying to make his way north across the Potomac. On January 19, 1865, Foote was allowed by the House to defend his attempted departure from the Confederacy. During the course of his remarks, he abused Akin severely. He eventually became so offensive that the Speaker of the House declared him out of order and forced him to discontinue his speech. Five days later a motion to expel him, which Akin supported, was lost because the vote fell one short of the required two-thirds. But a motion to censure, likewise supported by Akin, was adopted by a vote of 64 to 6. Foote later succeeded in departing the Confederacy and was then formally expelled from the House by unanimous vote.[22]

During the portion of his Congressional term covered by the

20. Coulter, *Confederate States*, 142.
21. Akin to his wife, Dec. 26, 1864.
22. Akin to his wife, Jan. 19, 20, 1865; Coulter, *Confederate States*, 135-36.

home letters here published, Akin lived in a Richmond boarding house run by George Washington Gretter, located about a quarter of a mile from the Capitol. His correspondence does not reveal what he had to pay for his meals and lodging, but after his pay was increased to $690 a month, he wrote that this amount would pay his expenses with "a little left to take home."[23] He described his room as large and simply, though comfortably, furnished The fare appears to have been ample in quantity, though the offerings frequently did not include dessert.

Owing to the loss of his home and much of his other property, and the high cost of living in Richmond and Elberton, Akin was constrained to practice rigid economy in all his activities. He repeatedly darned his own socks. To cut laundry expenses he wore the same shirt for three or four days, and night shirts and drawers were changed every two weeks. Socks, for which the laundry rate was $1 each, had to do a week's service between washings, and of handkerchiefs, the laundering cost of which was the same as socks, Akin wrote on January 14, 1865: "I carry and use my handkerchiefs until they are soiled so much I am ashamed to use them." High prices charged by cobblers caused Akin at considerable discomfort to put off unduly the resoling of his boots. All-in-all, his life in Richmond was a bleak and lonely existence. Even so, his lot was more tolerable than that of his wife, who had to endure the inconveniences and privations of a refugee in a land bedeviled by scarcity, high prices, fears of enemy invasion, and oppressed by ever-increasing realization of ultimate defeat. Mary Verdery Akin bore the responsibility for the welfare not only of her own small children but also of six or seven slaves who accompanied her to Elberton. Two of these she was able to hire out, after considerable difficulty. One other harassed her by a propensity for taking unauthorized leave. Her days were so full of activity and anxiety that she was completely exhausted at night. Little wonder that she could hardly find time to keep up a flow of correspondence with her absent husband.

Akin's letters reveal much about the man. One of his most

23. Akin to his wife, Dec. 29, 1864.

notable attributes was a deep interest in religion. He was an active member of the Methodist Church, a trustee of Emory College, and a local preacher. At least twice during his second session in Congress he preached to Georgia soldiers encamped near Richmond. His letters contain many references to religious matters, and reveal strong and abiding faith in God. Attending church services and listening to the sermons of the eminent ministers who filled Richmond pulpits were a principal source of enjoyment during his term in Congress.

He was a faithful husband and devoted father. His letters to his wife are replete with tender expressions of affection, and some of them are sprinkled with poetry. He was ever solicitous of the well-being of his children—their health, their religious training, their schooling, their habits, and their characters. He craved news of their sayings and small doings. He cherished their letters. And when his eldest son died near the end of the war, he was desolated by grief.

I. W. Avery, who was associated with Akin in public life and who knew him well, made the following comment about him and his career:

> He was a self-made man, possessing decided ability, and very effective speaking power, and as much purity of private character as any public man we have ever had in Georgia. He was a local methodist preacher. Col. Akin was rather a small man in physique, but had a voice of remarkable compass, both shrill and deep, with peculiar ringing quality in its high notes. He had unusual fervor and sincerity of conviction and earnestness of character. He could not be called a popular gentleman, on account of a certain unyielding vigor, and a forcible impatience at what he condemned. As a laborious student, in a clear comprehension of the law, and in strong argument, Col. Akin had no superior, and few equals in his circuit. No man in his section enjoyed a larger share of individual and public esteem than he. . . .[24]

A glimpse of Akin's modesty is afforded by the statement to

---

24. Avery, *History of the State of Georgia*, 95. Miss Sally May Akin, in a letter to Bell I. Wiley, September 7, 1956, stated concerning Avery's comments on the carrying power of her father's voice: "When he lived at Cassville he frequently preached at the Cassville Methodist Church. . . . I once met an old gentleman who knew father in those days and when I asked him if father was a good preacher he said: 'Yes, you could hear him a mile.' "

his wife in a letter of January 14, 1865: "If I spell any of my words wrong please tell me of it, and then it will save me from committing the mistake again." All-in-all he was an admirable character. The same may be said of his wife. Their reaction to the crisis of war, invasion, loss of home, separation, personal tragedy, defeat, and desolation mark them as people of great resourcefulness and strength.

After Lee's surrender, Akin returned to Bartow County where he resumed the practice of law. He died in Cartersville on December 17, 1877. He was survived by his wife Mary Verdery Akin who died on October 17, 1907; two daughters, Mary Verdery and Sally May; and four sons, Thomas Warren, John Wesley, Willie Edward, and Paul F. A daughter, Miss Sally May Akin, resides in St. Augustine, Florida. The last surviving son, Paul F. Akin, died on May 6, 1959, at Cartersville, Georgia, where for many years he had practiced law in the firm founded by his father. This firm continues under the direction of Warren Akin, son of Paul Akin.

* * * * *

The fifty letters here published comprise all that are known to be extant of Akin's Confederate correspondence. In some cases communications counted as a single letter actually are a series of communications extending over a period of several days but sent as one document. Thirty-four of the letters were written by Akin while he was a member of the Confederate Congress; all but one of these belong to the period of the second session of the Second Confederate Congress; and all but four were addressed to Akin's wife; one was to his daughter Kate; one to his son Elbert, and two to his good friend and neighbor Judge Nathan Land.

Six Akin letters of the pre-Congressional period—two to his wife and four to Nathan Land—are included for the light that they throw on his activities during the first years of the war.

Seven letters of Mrs. Akin to her husband, written in January and February, 1865, are reproduced because of what they tell of Akin's family and his relations with them, and because of the interesting and valuable information which they give concerning civilian life in an uninvaded area late in the conflict.

One post-war letter written by Akin to General S. B. Brown, commander of the occupation forces in the Elberton area, affords an interesting view of conditions and attitudes immediately following the conflict and tells something of the ex-Congressman's prewar sentiments. This letter was delivered by Amos T. Akerman, a friend of Akin's who was to achieve prominence in the Reconstruction period.

Two letters, one written to Mrs. Akin by B. C. Wall and the other a brief communication of Secretary of War James A. Seddon to Akin, are included for the glimpses which they give of Akin's business and legislative activities.

All of the letters except those addressed to Nathan Land (which are in the Georgia State Department of Archives and History) are in possession of Warren Akin of Cartersville. The story of how these letters came to the writer's attention illustrates the part that chance sometimes plays in historical research.

In 1953 I was invited to make a speech to the Cartersville Rotary Club. On that occasion I met Paul F. Akin, the Confederate Congressman's youngest son. I told him of my interest in Confederate Congressmen and asked him if he happened to have any of his father's war-time letters. He replied that he did not, and added that all the family's personal papers had been destroyed when the Federal forces burned the Akin home in 1864. About a year later, on a second speaking visit to the Cartersville Rotarians, I sat between Paul F. Akin and his son Warren. I was remarking to the former how sorry I was that all his father's war-time correspondence had been destroyed when Warren interrupted to state: "Why, Dad, not *all* the letters were lost. You turned over to me fifteen or twenty years ago a big batch of them. They are in a safe over at the office."

I was so excited that I probably shortened my speech. Immediately after the luncheon I went to the office of Akin and Akin, where father and son showed me the letters and generously permitted me to take them to Emory University for transcribing.

I am deeply grateful to them for permission to reproduce the letters and for help in digging out information about the Confederate Congressman and persons mentioned in the correspondence.

* * * * *

Paul F. Akin was right about the family papers being destroyed when the home was burned in 1864. But the letters here reproduced, with a few exceptions, are those written after Sherman's Georgia campaign. They are the more valuable because of the exceedingly great scarcity of Confederate Congressional correspondence during the final months of the conflict.

Sources used in preparing the introduction were: the Akin correspondence; personal interviews and correspondence with Paul F. Akin, supplemented by information provided by Miss Sally May Akin; manuscript census schedules for Cass and Elbert counties, 1860, in the National Archives, microfilm of which are available in the Georgia State Department of Archives and History; Lucy Josephine Cunyus, *History of Bartow County;* and a copy of a will, a biographical sketch and other miscellaneous materials in a small Warren Akin collection in the Georgia State Department of Archives and History.

These same sources were useful in identifying names mentioned in the correspondence. Also helpful for this purpose were microfilm in the Georgia Department of Archives and History of original muster rolls in the National Archives of Georgia units in the Confederate Army.

For valuable assistance in the laborious and time-consuming work of transcribing and proof-reading the letters and running down identifying data, I am indebted to my wife, Mary Frances Wiley, and to two former graduate assistants at Emory, May S. Ringold of Clemson College and Joseph T. Hatfield of Concord College. I wish also to make grateful acknowledgment of a research grant from Emory University, a part of which was used for this project.

The Akin letters, except those in the last chapter, were published serially in the *Georgia Historical Quarterly*, March, 1958-September, 1959. I am indebted to E. Merton Coulter, editor of the *Quarterly*, for permission to reprint the material.

Bell Irvin Wiley

☆ 1 ☆

"If We Ever Have Another Boy . . . I Will Call Him Bartow"

Richmond Va. [25th]
July 24th/1861.

MY DEAR WIFE: I now commence my fourth letter to you, and to say I am *anxious* to hear from you feebly expresses my feelings. O how much pleasure it would afford me to know you and all the dear ones were well. I am happy to inform you that the four Georgia companies reported killed or taken prisoners at Laurel Hill are all safe. I saw one of the captains—Capt Ezzard[25] of Atlanta—this evening. He has just left my room. He & Ralph Banks heard I was here and came to see me. Banks is from Monroe Co. & Lieut. in Capt. Pinckard's company,[26] from Monroe—(also reported lost.) and is a brother of Elbert Banks living near Mr. Fambrough's. Capt Ezzard is going home & will take this & either leave it at Cass Station or mail it close by, so you will get it much soon[er] than by mail.

Prest. Davis returned to Richmond last night bringing 675 prisoners. A large crowd gathered around the Hotel (Spottswood) where he is staying and called for him vociferously. He went to the window & made them a speech. I was at the Hotel in Judge Nisbet's[27] room & went in to the Presidents parlor & heard the speech and had an in-

25. Captain William L. Ezzard, Co. "F" ("Gate City Guards") 1st (Ramsey's) Georgia Regt. See Franklin M. Garrett, *Atlanta and Environs* (New York, 1854), I, 500.

26. Co. "K" 1st (Ramsey's) Ga. Regt., commanded by Capt. James S. Pinckard of Forsyth, Ga. This information is from microfilm in Ga. State Department of Archives and History of original muster rolls in National Archives. Except when otherwise indicated all identifying information on military personnel given in subsequent references is from this source.

27. Eugenius A. Nisbet, Georgia state supreme court justice, 1845-1853, and member of Confederate Provisional Congress. Allen Johnson and Dumas Malone, eds. *Dictionary of American Biography* (New York, 1928), xiii, 527-528 cited hereafter as *DAB*. The *DAB* sketch states that Nisbet declined election to the Provisional Congress, but the *Executive and Congressional Directory of the Confederate States 1861-1865* (Washington, 1899) lists him as a member. Moreover, *The Journal of the Confederate States of America, 1861-1865* (Washington, 1904-1905. I, shows that Nisbet was attending the sessions of Congress during July, 1861.

troduction to him after the speech. Chesnutt[28] of So. Ca. made a speech also. The president looks thin & feeble, but his wife is a fine, good-looking lady with a plenty of flesh & blood.

Today the death of Bartow[29] was formally announced in Congress by the Hon. Tom Cobb.[30] His remarks were feeling & beautiful. Ben Hill,[31] Mason of Va.[32] & Chesnutt of S. C. made speeches & Congress adjourned. After Bartow's 8th Ga. Regt. was much cut to pieces late in the day, he rode to Genl Beauregard and said: "What is now to be done Direct me and it shall be done if within human power." Beauregard replied, "That battery must be taken." Bartow immediately rallied the remnant of the 8th & ordered the 7th Georgia & one Va. Regt. with the 8th to take it. The charge was made & soon Bartow's horse was shot under him & he wounded in the leg. He then went from company to company, cheering the men & officers onward, telling them "the day is ours; onward and take the battery." When within forty yards of the battery, (which was manned & supported by U. S. *Regulars*) the standard bearer was shot down. Bartow seized the colors, waived it over his head with his cap in his hand waiving it also and bidding his men to follow him—his men falling at every discharge from the battery, almost like wheat stalks before the scyth, - and just then a bullet pierced his breast. A few of his men gathered around their fallen Genl. & colours, and he said to them, "they have killed me, but the day is ours. Never give up the field." In a few moments the brave *volunteers* took the battery & the U. S. *regulars* were routed and fled from the field. What bravery and unfaltering intrepidity was displayed by the gallant Georgians. All honor to them. Peace to the fallen brave, and green will be their memory in the hearts of freemen while Liberty has a votary or freedom a defender. While our hearts bleed for lost ones, we can but pray God's blessing on the heart-stricken bereaved ones, over all our beloved Georgia. If we ever have another boy, I now feel like I will call him Bartow.[33] He told his wife when he left her here that he did not expect to return, and if he did die he wanted to die on the battle field fighting for Southern liberty. He did die and at the place de-

28. James Chesnut, member of the Provisional Confederate Congress from South Carolina and later aide to Jefferson Davis. *DAB*, IV, 58.

29. Brig. Gen. Francis S. Bartow, member of the Confederate Provisional Congress from Ga., killed at First Manassas, July 21, 1861.

30. Thomas R. R. Cobb, member of Confederate Provisional Congress from Georgia. For resolutions of tribute to Bartow, introduced by Cobb and unanimously adopted by Congress, see *Journal of Confed. Cong.*, I, 280-81.

31. Benjamin Harvey Hill, prominent Georgia statesman, member of Confederate Provisional Congress and later Confederate Senator.

32. James M. Mason, Confederate Congressman and diplomat.

33. Akin changed his mind as none of the sons afterward born to him was named for Bartow.

sired. He left no children. He had an adopted son who was badly, if not fatally wounded in the same fight.

It is said that the Yankees are catching all the negroes they can and are sending and selling them in Cuba.[34] It might be well to let ours know this, but not let them know your reason. Tell Mrs. Land to do the same. Do not let this be put where it may be read by any one but you. You may let Judge Land[35] read it.

I expect to leave here in a few days & stop at Whit[e] Sulpher Springs for a few days. There is such a crowd here that it is difficult to do any thing. No one is still permitted to go to Manasses & will not be soon. Fathers brothers & others are here trying to get permission to go and see about their loved ones, but in vain. Boling & Joe Stovall came here to-day, but I have not seen them. I have been to their room & sent there twice, but they were not in.

I inclose you a note for Mrs. Saxon.[36] He says send it by one of the little boys.

I will be at home some day next week.

God bless you all.

Your devoted husband

Milledgeville, Nov. 24th 1862.

MY DEAR WIFE: I wrote you a few lines yesterday and as I have no company to-night I commence another letter. I am *so* anxious to see you. It seems to me I never was so desireous to see you before. Now, if your health is sufficient and your wardrobe in condition, I would be delighted for you to come down here about the 5th or 6th of December.[37] You could start on Friday morning and reach Macon that evening about sunset. Stay all night there and reach here next day at three oclock P. M. I could meet you at Macon & come back with you Sun. You could bring Rachal or Emily[38] with you—(Rachal I reckon would suit best,) and stay here until the 16th & then we would leave here in the morning and get home that night. But I fear your health will not allow it. Think about it and write me what you will do. You could leave all the other children at home

34. The erroneous report that the Federals were seizing Negroes and sending them to Cuba had wide circulation in the Confederacy. See Bell Irvin Wiley, *Southern Negroes, 1861-1865* (New Haven, 1938), 13-14.

35. Judge Nathan Land and his wife, as previously noted, were friends and neighbors of the Akins.

36. The Saxons apparently were Cassville neighbors of the Akins.

37. At the time this letter was written Akin was in Milledgeville, then state capital of Georgia, serving in the legislature.

38. Rachel and Emily were family slaves who helped Mrs. Akin care for her children.

and get Miss Nancy McTier or Harriet Land[39] to stay with them. If you come of course Elbert and Warren cannot.[40] I[f] you can not come I would like for the boys to come very much. They could leave home in the morning and reach here that night at one oclock. Stay a few days and return home. I know they would be much pleased and instructed by their visit. The Lunatic Assylum and the Penitentiary would be very interesting to them. I could take time to go with them to these places and show them everything of interest. There is a cotton factory here where they spin and weave cloth of several kinds, and this too would be interesting to them. I could have seats furnished them in the Hall of the House and they could spend a few days profitably in looking on the Legislature in transacting business.

Tuesday evening–Since writing the foregoing I have purchased an ounce of calomel and will inclose same in this letter. I am trying to get some vaccine virus to inclose also, and, if I send it, have my whole family, black and white, vaccinated at once. It will take but a small quantity to serve for all. Have each one vaccinated in three or four places, so that if one place fails another may have the desired effect. I will try and obtain the vaccine matter during the afternoon so that it may go off in this letter; but I fear I will fail.

I see in the papers that rock salt has been discovered near Opelika Ala. and I saw a specimen of the salt this morning, and was told that there were 1000 hands at work there making salt. "It is most too good to be true," but I hope it is. I will know in a few days. I must stop and go to the House, as it is nearly three oclock.

I inclose some vaccine virus. Have all vaccinated, and give the remainder to Dr. Hardy. If any of those vaccinated takes well try and not have the scab broken, but preserve it whole and when it comes off put it in a paper and then in a vial & stop with bees-wax.

I have much to say to you but must hasten in order to get this in the mail.

My dear darling do write me often at least every other day.

Love and a kiss, to all the dear ones

Your devoted husband

---

39. Nancy McTier and Harriet Land were friends and neighbors of the Akins.

40. Elbert and Warren were sons of Warren Akin whose ages in November, 1862, were 13 and 11 respectively.

Oxford Ga. March 25/64

[To Nathan Land][41]

MY DEAR SIR: Yours of the 24th inst was received this morning. I was glad to hear from you, but very sorry to learn you are not more actively employed. If you were constantly engaged you would not have time to become unhappy. Doing nothing, the mind has time to be miserable. I am writing you now, not because I feel like it but because I have nothing to do. I feel like sleeping not writing. I did not sleep much last night. My dear little Mary is very ill.[42] I have had two physicians attending her for several days, and this morning they suggested the propriety of sending for a third, and I done so. They all admit they do not know what is the matter with her. She blistered on the breast, but is the most quiet child, all things considered, I ever saw. She seems to be in great pain at times, but when easy she sometimes sings, with much strength. Lying in bed last night she commenced singing like she did some times when well. Since the blister was drawn she has seemed more at herself, not so much in a stupor, but she has manifested a much keener sense of pain. She is now quiet, is sleeping, but I fear she has a chill, as her feet are cold. What is to be the result, how I am to be afflicted, God only knows. But he doeth all things well. He has taken three of my children[43] to Heaven and if it is his will to take my darling little Mary from me, I hope he will give me grace to bear it. He gave her to me and he has the right to take her again. I try to pray for her restoration to health, but I pray for His will, not mine, to be done. The doctors say she is not dangerous, but I think differently. The little thing has suffered much. Her pulse has ranged from 130 to 160 per minute. How painful - how terribly distressing it is to see her suffering, and be totally unable to give any relief. I may be able to give you more deffinite information about her before this is mailed, as it is now too late to send it off today. Warren is sick and has fever this evening. I fear he is going to be sick.

Saturday. I don't know whether my dear little daughter is any

---

41. Nathan Land, born in Twiggs County, May 11, 1812, was a resident and prominent citizen of Cassville from 1848 until his death in 1880. In the 1850's he was judge of the inferior court of his county and during the Civil War he held the office of ordinary. When the Federals approached Cassville he refugeed to Brooks County. The invaders burned his home "Cassville Heights." The Lands and the Akins were neighbors and friends.

42. Mary Verdery Akin was three years old at this time. She recovered and lived until 1942.

43. The three deceased children were all boys. George, born Sept. 12, 1853, died Dec. 13, 1853; Augustus Verdery, born Dec. 30, 1854, died June 10, 1857; Henry Clay, born Aug. 13, 1857, died Sept. 19, 1860. Information provided by Paul F. Akin, from family records.

better. All of the doctors came to see her this morning. One of them said he thought she was better. The others gave no opinion. Warren is sick - had high fever all night and pain in his side. I think he has pneumonia, and fear he will have a bad time of it, but hope for the best. I am not well. I have taken something as medicine nearly every day since you saw me. I am now suffering from pain in my back side & legs. But it is all right, and I hope will work for my good. I have very little hope that my little daughter will recover, though she may do so. The doctors say they think she will. If she dies I expect to carry her body home to be buried & will write you to have a grave dug. God, in his mercy, wisdom & love, grant that you may be saved this trouble. If I did not believe in God's overruling and protecting love, I know not what I should do now. But I know he does nothing wrong or unkind, and he will take care of me I believe. If he takes all of my children, it will be exactly right, however my poor heart may fail and grieve. Neither my wife or myself has had a good night's sleep this week, and she is nearly worn out watching & nursing.

I am sorry to hear you are unnecessarily making yourself unhappy. You do not believe in God as you ought. Because you think you failed to make a few dollars, that can never make you happy in time or eternity. You are grieving and fretting - when, perhaps, God prevented you making the trade for your good. He says "*all* things *shall* work together for good to them that love" him and yet you say, this is not true, or you admit you do not love him, lest he chasten you most sorely. You know you once sold your place and how much you suffered for it, and God permitted you to suffer until you returned to it. You have lived there long and never lost a child, and had you sold it again you know not what you might have suffered for it. I have no doubt, if you had sold your place and went to the Dukes place, you would have been very unhappy about it. And what if you did lose a few thousand in Confederate notes, what does it amount to? How long will you need them? If you will resolve, by God's grace to be contented and cheerful, let what may happen, and then go to him in secret prayer at least once a day, and pray for a cheerful & cont[ent]ed spirit, see if you are not happier. Try it, and I think you will not only be happier, but all around you will be. Try God and see if he does not bless you. But you must do your part, trust God & stop grieving. I cant write more now. Yours truly Warren Akin

If I can get a box I will send you some potatoes Monday.

Oxford, April 4th 1864

[To Nathan Land]

DEAR SIR: My children are a great deal better. But Mary cannot yet speak. The strangest case I ever saw. If they get no worse I will be at Manassas[44] Wednesday evening to attend to arbitrating a case on thursday for Bro. Weems.[45] If I fail to get there, please say to him my children are too sick to leave them is the cause of my absence. I expect to go up on the accommodation train and will stop at your house.

If I do not get there, and bro Weems' adversary will wait a few days I may still go up. Or if they will come down here I will attend to the case here.

If I am not up at the time mentioned, you may know that one or both of my children are worse. Yours truly

44. After secession, Akin and his neighbors tried to change the name of their town from Cassville—which had become objectionable owing to the original honoree, Lewis Cass, being a Yankee—to Manassas. The new name did not gain official recognition. But Akin was successful in changing the name of the county from Cass to Bartow, the name being selected in honor of the hero of First Manassas.

45. This is probably A. J. Weems, listed in the 1860 census as a minister of Cassville.

☆ 2 ☆

"We Are Getting on Very Slowly"

April 10th 1864

[To Nathan Land]

MY DEAR FRIEND: I did not reach home until yesterday.[46] Friday morning when waked up to start it was raining so hard I thought it best not to turn out. I came down on the eleven oclock train on friday and stopped at Allatoona and staid at Mr Latimer's until Saturday morning. What a pitiful sight he is. His nose all gone up to the bone, his gums in front and the palate of his mouth all gone & his upper front teeth fallen out. He is very much emaciated, & had not had an action on his bowels for forty two days. The night I staid there the oil he had taken acted. He says he is *ready* and only waiting the summons. What an awful condition he is in. How thankful I am that God has spared me such an affliction.

When I arrived here yesterday evening, I found my children greatly improved - my little daughter in the piazza saying before I reached her "father, father." O how my poor heart swelled with inexpressible joy to hear [her] speak again. I felt that God had given me back my child - that my prayers had been heard and answered. She seemed almost like one raised from the dead. I took her in my arms, pressed her to my heart, while tears of gratitude flowed free and fast. How good God is to me. Every day, every hour I am receiving blessings from him. O Lord, make me more thankful! Warren has greatly improved, but his mouth is very sore and he can eat only with trouble and some pain. I think both my children will soon be well. Mary can sit up, and I think will be walking in a few days. She improves rapidly. She is the most quiet, patient and affectionate child I ever saw. She does not fret or cry about any thing. It is very difficult for her to speak many words yet, and her efforts to talk are sometimes distressing to witness. But my children are getting well! Thank God! Thank God!

I took dinner with Mr Solomon yesterday. Had a good dinner - they were all well. His health seemed to be better, I think, than common. He inquired after you very kindly.

46. This letter, presumably like that of April 4, was written from Oxford, Georgia, where the Akin family was temporarily residing.

I saw some of the new issue of Confederate notes yesterday, and I suppose they will soon take the place of the old notes. I gave $150 of the old for $100. of the new issue, the old change bills will now come out again, and soon the old issue will be out of circulation altogether.

I asked, not long since, in a letter to a gentleman of your acquaintance, what he thought of Wrights resolutions,[47] & the suspension of the writ of Habeas Corpus[48] &c. He replied that Wright's resolutions are "the treacherous out-cropping of a tory substratum, that the suspension of the writ was like a certain other *suspension*, terrible to traitors only." A member of congress from Kentucky told me yesterday that Wright would have been expelled from congress if he had not left Richmond so suddenly. I am glad he left and prevented another topic for exciting news-paper articles. We ought to avoid every thing that may produce a difference of opinion and a division among the people, if it be possible.

Monday- . My little daughter is still improving. Warren is not doing so well. His mouth is very sore, and his face is swelled. I hope, however, he will soon be able to go to school.

Have you any turnip seed? If so send me some by mail.

I hope that box will get here soon for my potatoes are rotting very fast. The cold weather injured them and they will soon be gone.

In two weeks more, God permitting, I will leave for Richmond,[49] and I will be glad to hear from you when I get there.

My kind respects to all your family Yours truly

Warren Akin

Elberton Ga.

October 31st 1864

[To Nathan Land]

MY DEAR SIR, Your very welcome letter of the 21st inst. is received. It is now a little after day-break, my boys & negroes are gone ten miles into the country to pick peas, and I am writing to you. Times are tight, family increasing, and it behooves me to be stirring. We

47. This was probably the resolution introduced in the Confederate House of Representatives on February 3, 1864 by Augustus R. Wright of Georgia, proposing a meeting between delegates of North and South to consider the establishment of a government "founded upon the integrity and sovereignty of the states." See *Journal of Confed. Cong.*, VI, 738.

48. Congress, on Davis' strong plea, in February 1864, voted to renew suspension of the writ of habeas corpus, for the period February 15-August 1, 1864. This act aroused a storm of protest. See Coulter, *The Confederate States*, 394-95.

49. The second session of the Second Confederate Congress was to convene on November 7, 1864.

have another daughter, born on the 28th inst.[50] Mother & child doing very well; but I am very fearful Mrs Akin's breasts are going to give her much trouble. How we do miss Mrs. Land! Indeed, we miss *all* your family, *all the time*. O how glad I shall be, if my life be spared, when the time comes for us all to go back to our old homes. For it will come some day. How *very* pleasant [it] is to meet with one just out from Cassville. As I came here I saw Bill Aycock[51] & Tom Word[52] on their way to Cassville. Aycock has returned. Ben Godfrey has seen him and learned many things of interest, if I could remember them & had time to write them. Aycock staid in the county some ten days. Tom Word is there yet. On the night of the 23rd inst. George Cobb[53] and Charly Goodwin staid with me. The latter just out from Cassville. The news obtained from him and Aycock was worth to me many newspapers. The Yankees came up from Kingston and drove off Mrs. Browns cows. Miss Mollie & another girl followed them and out in the road near McTier's place they came in sight of them. The girls on a hill and the Yankees in a bottom below. The girls clapped their hands, and screamed out at the top of their voice, "here they are, catch them, catch them," and the Yankees thought our scouts were after them, ran off & left the cows, and the girls drove them back home. There are but five men in Cassville, Sylar, Holmes, Nelson, Jo. Day & Tom Word.[54] Mrs Kirkham has gone to Nashville and carried all of Levy's furniture with her.[55] Mrs Stepp is living in George Gilreath's house, and riding about in my carriage administering to the wants of the poor! ! ![56] Dr Griffin[57] is living at Pittard's place. Mrs. Gaines & Lizzy are at Buford's place. There is a man, named Vaughan, living at Munford's place, and commanding a company of "home guards", (tories) He captured one of A. J. Weems sons, and one of the Windsor's and put them in irons,

50. The new baby was Susie Henry Akin. She died in 1871.

51. This was probably William L. Aycock of Cassville, listed in the 1860 census as a deputy sheriff.

52. Probably Thomas A. Word of Cassville, listed as a clerk in the 1860 census.

53. Probably George S. Cobb, listed in the 1860 census as a Cassville clerk.

54. These were presumably Cassville residents who remained during the Federal occupation or who returned after Hood began his raids in Sherman's rear in early October, 1864. Sylar was probably William Sylar, a carpenter and Holmes, H. H. Holmes, a carriage manufacturer. Nelson and Joe Day could not be identified in the 1860 census.

55. Mrs. Kirkham was probably the wife of Robert Kirkham, Cass County farmer. Levy may have been Samuel Levy; his occupation is not given in the 1860 census.

56. Mrs. Stepp was probably the wife of Joseph Stepp, Cass County farmer, and Gilreath, George H. Gilreath, also a farmer and a local Methodist preacher.

57. Dr. C. M. Griffin of Cassville.

and they were thus sent off to Chattanooga. Our scouts made diligent search for Vaughan, afterwards, but he kept closely at Cartersville. Sylar & Nelson went to the Yankees & reported themselves Union men. Holmes went with them. He told the Yankees that he voted against secession just as Sylar and Nelson did; but when Georgia seceded he seceded, that all his interest was with Georgia, and he expected it ever to remain so. Mrs. Wyly[58] is living with Jim Hones, at Cartersville. Mrs McMurray[59] is living in the house that Saxon formerly owned. Walker[60] has returned and is staying up at his father's making shoes. Bogh is a good rebel, and his daughter as full of rebel blood as a tick. They call themselves "rebels," and those who have "Union" proclivities, they call "home made Yankees." Bob Russell's[61] supply of whiskey is cut short and he has become quite lean. Aycock & Word went first into the sixth district, and got some one to go down with them nearly to Cassville. They went through the woods, and when near Bob Russell's they sent the man to his house & he told him there were two men out in the woods, who wanted to see him & wanted something to eat, but did not tell their names. Bob fixed up a blue bucket of food and started to them & when he got near them and saw it was Tom Word & Bill Aycock, he was so much surprised & rejoiced he let his bucket fall & emptied out all the victuals. Some man, whose name I have forgotten, saw Aycock up in the 6th and put his wife on a horse and sent her to Kingston to let the Yankees know he had come in, & they were soon after him, and came near catching him twice. He staid up in the 6th most of the time, and while he was sleeping one day a few Yankees rode up to the gate. Mrs Aycock went out, and they asked her if any rebels had passed there recently. She replied "Yes, some passed here a few minutes since." "How many were there" asked the Yankees? "I dont know" said Mrs. Aycock "but suppose there were about forty of them." This alarmed the few Yankees and they turned and rode off as fast as they could. Branson[62] has gone back home. Aycock was at his house, and took a nap of sleep there, and while he slept Mrs. B. kept watch for him. The most of the people are true "rebels" and will d[i]vide, with gladness, the last mouthful of

58. Probably William Clark Wyly, or Augustine Clayton Wyly, both of whom served as justice of the peace in Cass County in the 1850's, according to Cunyus, *History of Bartow County*, 105.

59. Possibly the wife of Madison McMurray, Cassville merchant.

60. Probably F. M. Walker, listed in the 1860 census as a Cassville bootmaker.

61. The only Robert Russel found in the 1860 census for Cass County was a 35-year-old farmer.

62. Possibly Levy Bransin, a Cass County farmer.

bread with a rebel soldier. Hank is a "rebel," and will carry food five miles into the mountains to feed a rebel scout.

The Yankees have destroyed many houses. Wolley's and Bro. Bests have been torn down.[63] They have recently destroyed nearly everything Sylar had. Goodwin & some twenty others charged into the rear guard of about 150 Yankees near Miles' residence on the Tenn. Road. They captured five or six, killed about the same number, and carried off some horses. For this, the Yankees returned and burnt up Miles house. About the fourteenth inst. our scouts attacked the guard of a "medicine wagon," captured the guard, wagon & medicine & killed one white & one black Yankee. This was near the "Cherokee Baptist College."[64] The next day the Yankees returned and burnt the Male College, Dr Rambant's house, and your dwelling.[65] (Well, breakfast is over, the sun is up and I can now see to write without the aid of a candle, and resume my pen.)

I regret to have to write you such bad news, and thought once, I would let you find it out from some other source; but I could not write you without informing you. Your house has shared the same fate a great many others have. But we have the consolation of knowing we will not need houses long, - troubles will soon be past, and if faithful unto the end, we will soon have "a house not made with hands," and one that cannot be destroyed by enemies. And there is another consoling reflection, full of comfort in these troublous times. If we are God's children the burning of our houses "*shall* work" for *our good*. We cant see how it is, but it *is so*, I do not have a doubt of it. And there is still another comforting reflection. If we are righteous our children will never be seen "begging bread," even though all our worldly substances may be destroyed. Cheer up, then, and press onward, and look upward.

Many of our boys have been back to Cassville. Among them Jim Kinney and Bill Light. When the latter reached there he found his

---

63. Hezekiah Best, planter and local Methodist preacher, who migrated to Cass County from Maryland in 1857 and acquired a large estate on Two Run Creek, known as "Forest Home." His property included a grist mill, gin and saw mill. See Cunyus, *History of Bartow County*, 47. Wolley could not be identified.

64. This institution, operating under the auspices of the Cherokee Baptist Convention, was a men's college established in 1854. Cunyus, *History of Bartow County*, 144-47.

65. Thomas Rambant was president of the Cherokee Baptist College. The Male College must have been the Cherokee Baptist College, as Cassville seems to have had no other men's college at this time. Possibly Akin used the term to distinguish this institution from the Cassville Female College sponsored by the Methodists. See Dorothy Orr, *History of Education in Georgia* (Chapel Hill, 1950), 154, and Cunyus, *History of Bartow County*, 141-44.

mother at Kingston among the Yankees, and he was greatly outraged in feeling. He is said to be as gallant a young man as ever drew a sword. Jim Kinney shot and killed one of the provost guard at Athens as the boys returned back. Several of the boys were on a spree and the guard was ordered to arrest them. He arrested one, and Kinney walked up to him and said he is my friend, drew his pistol and shot him. The guard died that night, and Kinney is in the hands of the authorities. I have not heard what has been done, but expect to hear that the soldiers have turned him loose.

Godfrey told me some one had taken your furniture and carried it to his house in the country. The Yankees tore up every thing Mrs McMurray had, and treated Mrs. Hanks[66] the same way.

While the skirmish was going on across our town several women & children were in the cellar of Bohannon, - among them old Mrs Armstead.[67] While the cannon were booming the children commenced crying and their screaming annoyed Mrs Armstead very much. She finally could stand it no longer, and rushing out of the cellar she declared she would "risk the bullets before she would stand all that squalling." I think this decidedly the most laughable thing I have heard, connected with home folks, since I left Cassville. Cant you see the old lady, as she rushes up the cellar door declaring that the squalling of the children are more terrible to her than Yankee bullits and shells. I would like to hear her description of *that* battle.

The 20th Army Corps (Yankee) marched through Cassville towards Rome on the 16th inst.

Your brotherinlaw's land was given to relieve him from military service to the Confederate States. It was not understood or intended to shield him from any militia duty to the State, nor any other duty, patrol, jury or road duty. The State has as much right to call him from home to perform militia duty as any other duty. The Confederate States Government could not relieve him from duty to the State, if it wished to do so. If it could relieve the citizen from *one* duty to the State, it might from every one, and thus destroy the State Government. It may exempt the citizen from military duty to the Confederate States, but it can not exempt him from discharging his duty of the State. Neither can the State exempt the citizen from his duty to the Confederate States, for if this could be done the State could destroy the Confederate Government while remaining a member of the Confederate Government. You will see at once, therefore,

66. Probably Elizabeth Hanks, Cassville landlady.

67. The census of 1860 lists two Cassville Bohannons, R. Bohannon, a harness maker, and W. Bohannon, a day laborer. Mrs. Armstead could not be identified.

that no one who has given bond, and obtained an exemption, under the Act of Congress, from military service to the Confederate States, has any just cause of complaint because he has to perform any duty he may owe the State. He might be exempted from performing jury duty to the Confederate States, but this would not discharge him from similar duty to the State. He might be exempted from paying taxes to the Confederate States, but the State could still rightfully collect tax from him. The principle is the same in each case, though differing in degree and kind. These things originate in the complex nature of our Government, and cannot be avoided. Let your brother-inlaw know these views. He will see, at once, their force and may relieve his mind from what he now thinks is a hardship.

As to calling out the negro men and placing them in the army, with the promise that they shall be free at the end of the war, I can only say it is a question of fearful magnitude. Can we prevent subjugation, confiscation, degradation and slavery without it. If not, will our condition or that of the negro, be any worse by calling them into service.[68]

On the other hand: Can we feed our soldiers and their families if the negro men are taken from the plantations? Will our soldiers submit to having our negroes along side them in the ditches, or in line of battle? When the negro is taught the use of arms and the art of war, can we live in safety with them afterwards? Or if it be contemplated to send them off to another country, when peace is made, will it be right to force them to a new, distant and strange land, after they have fought for and won the independence of this? Would they go without having another war? Involving, perhaps a general insurrection of all the negroes? To call forth the negroes into the army, with the promise of freedom, will it not be giving up the great question involved by doing the very thing Lincoln is now doing? The Confederate States may take private property for public use, by paying for it; but can we ever pay for 300,000 negro men at present prices, in addition to our other indebtedness? The Confederate Government may buy the private negro property of the Citizens, but can it set them free among us, to corrupt our slaves, and place in peril our existence? These are some of the thoughts that have passed th[r]ough my mind on the subject. But I can not say that I have a definite and fixed opinion. If I were convinced that

68. The question of making soldiers of slaves caused controversy in Congress and throughout the Confederacy in the last six months of the war. Finally on March 13, 1865 President Davis was authorized to call on the states for as many as 300,000 Negro soldiers, but only a few of those recruited under this act got into uniform and none of them went into battle. See Wiley, *Southern Negroes 1861-1865*, 146-62.

we will be subjugated, with the long train of horrors that will follow it, unless the negroes be placed in the army, I would not hesitate to enrol our slaves and put them to fighting. Subjugation will give us free negroes in abundance - enemies at that - while white slaves will be more numerous than free negroes. We and our children will be slaves, while our freed negroes will lord it over us. It is impossible for the evils resulting from placing our slaves in the army to be greater than those that will follow subjugation. We may (if necessary) put our slaves in the army, win our independence, and have liberty and homes for ourselves and children. But subjugation will deprive us of our homes, houses, property, liberty, honor, and every thing worth living for, leaving for us and our posterity only the chains of slavery, tenfold more galling and degrading than that now felt by our negroes. But I will not enlarge, I have made suggestions merely for your reflection.

Have you ever noticed the strange conduct of our people during this war? They give up their sons, husbands, brothers & friends, and often without murmuring, to the army; but let one of their negroes be taken, and what a houl you will hear. The love of money has been the greatest difficulty in our way to independence, - it is now our chief obstacle. "For the love of money is the root of all evil; which while some coveted after they have erred from the faith, and pierced themselves through with many sorrows." What a fearful realizing of this truth many will feel after this war. Their hearts will be "pierced through with many sorrows."

I think you ought to stay in Brooks. Do not leave it to your girls. They can not look to the future and act from Judgement as you can. Girls, like too many men, look to present comfort and enjoyment too often; and while your daughters would say that which they believed to be best, yet they are not calculated to decide like you and Mrs. Land. God bless them, I do sympathize with them and want to see them very much. Give them my kind respects when you write them. I think I will write to them before a great while.

You ought not to be troubled about John's being in the army. You cant avoid it, and it is not wise to complain. "Rejoice always, And *in every thing give thanks*." How much worse his and your condition might be. In twelve months more Elbert will be sixteen years old, and I may then have to send him forth into militia service. I dont think I will grieve about it. Better go at once and help to win independence than stay home and live a long life of slavery.

I know we will rejoice and thank God when we get back in peace to our old homes. But troubles will not then have ended. They will never end here. It is only through tribulation we can enter into heaven. We must have troubles and trials here. "But count it all joy when ye fall into divers temptation; knowing this that the trying of your faith worketh patience. But let patience have her perfect work, that ye may be perfect and entire, wanting nothing." There is much comfort and encouragement to the tried troubled soul in the following lines of one of our beautiful hymns by Cowper:

"Trials must, and will befall;
But with humble faith to see
Love inscribed upon them all, -
This is happiness to me.
Trials make the promise sweet;
Trials give new life to prayer;
Bring me to my Saviour's feet,
Lay me low, and keep me there."

I intend to write to John, but do not know how to direct my letter.

Congress meets next Monday, the 7th proximo (Nov[r].) But I can not leave home until Mrs. Akin is able to leave her bed. So you may write me again to this place. I will write you when I leave for Richmond.

We are among very kind people here. They have aided in feeding us to a great extent since we have been here. I do not remember whether I wrote you how many things my friends had given me, and will now do so. One has sent me a cow to milk, two hams, thirty pounds lard and some butter - sent at least twenty miles. Another sent us some beef, butter, a bag of sweet and one of Irish potatoes, and a dimijohn of syrup, and jeans for a pair of pants. Another sent us seven pounds butter; another two pounds; and a lady [sent] jeans for a suit of clothes; and a number of other things of less importance, but of real value to us, and one gives me all my firewood. I have to pay eight hundred dollars rent for the lot we are on - having about seven acres of land, - five of which I expect to put in wheat or corn. We have some fruit trees on the place and a well of excellent water.

Tell James & Freeman that Elbert and Warren have no school now, and they get up every morning, before day, and go ten miles into the country and gather a wagon load of peas and return home about eight oclock at night, sometimes. This is their amusement. I bought wool hats for them recently at twenty dollars each, and nine yards of jeans at twelve dollars a yard. But I will not bore you longer. Pardon my many *words*. When I commence writing to you I feel like I'm talking to you, and I hurry on without stoping to think much. Present me kindly to all your family. Mrs Akin is anxiously looking for a letter from Mrs. Land. She sends love to all

Yours truly
Warren Akin

Please let Dr Verdery know how we all are, and present him our respects

W. A.

Richmond Va.
Nov. 28th 1864

MY DEAR WIFE I reached here last night after nine oclock, had no mishap on the way, and am quite well and now in my seat. I was just 9½ hours going from Greensboro N. C. to Danville Va. a distance of 48 miles, travelled in a box car in the night and slept on some corn sack, but as it was not very cold, I made out pretty well.[69] I am boarding for the present at the American Hotel, and have to pay $25 per day for board, and one dollar every time my boots are blacked, and $10 per dozen or $30 per month for washing. So my board will be at least $810 per month, and if I am here long it will take all my pay to meet expenses travelling to and from this place and while here, - even if it will meet them. I know not how long I am to support my family, if this war continues long. Everything I have been working hard for for so many years will be *eaten up* and in my old age myself family and children will be left without the means of support. But I will try and trust Him who "tempers the wind to the shorn lamb," and do the best I can. I wish you would, some pleasant day, have hitched one of the mules to the buggy and ride out to see Mr. Tate[70] and ask him to let me have some twenty acres of land to cultivate in corn next year, and some ten or fifteen acres to sow in oats. Do your best on him—tell him how necessary it is for us etc. etc.

I found here this morning a large number of letters, which I have not had time to read. Two came by flag of Truce, and one from Miss Callie Lane. I have not time to write you much *now,* will write again soon. I did not get up this morning until a short time before 9 oclock, having lost so much sleep on the way here. I slept from the time I got to bed, or soon there after, until just before eight oclock this morning, and did not get to breakfast until after nine oclock. I then had my hair trimmed, and did not get here until a few

69. Akin's travel difficulties were not unusual for this period, owing to the deterioration and poor management of railroad facilities. See Robert C. Black, *The Railroads of the Confederacy* (Chapel Hill, 1952), 214-95.
70. Probably U. O. Tate, Elbert County farmer.

minutes before twelve, and I now write while business is being transacted, that my letter may leave by first mail. Tell *all* my children, even to Kate,[71] to write me. and kiss *all* for me.

I have much to write, but no time *now*.

Write me by *every mail*.

Your devoted husband
Warren Akin

Sunday. Richmond, Va.
Decr 11th 1864.

MY DEAR WIFE: I went down at 9½ oclock this morning, to attend prayer meeting at the Senate chamber, and received your short note of the 2nd inst. Short as it was, I am very glad to get it. I have written you several letters, telling you every thing, how I got on coming here, where I am boarding etc. etc. I suppose Elbert told you who he saw in Abbeville. Mrs. Banton came from Abbeville to Greensboro N. C. and I had her in charge and, therefore, obtained a seat in the ladies car that far. From Greensboro to Danville I travelled in a box car. It was night, and I had a corn sack for my bed and another for my pillow. I[t] was not cold and I slept pretty well. I was nine hours and a half travelling in that way 48 miles. But I experienced no inconvenience from it. Since I have been here it has been very warm, and I have had some cold, but not "bad" as we usually say. It did not interfere at all with my meals or my duties, and I am quite well now, except a little cold. Heard Dr. Duncan preach this morning, a most excellent sermon.[72] I wish you could hear him. He is one of the most agreeable and pleasant speakers I ever listened to.

We had some snow here friday night and a little sleet with it, and yesterday the ground was covered in white and the trees hanging with ice. It grew warmer and the snow melted rapidly and most of them are gone, and the streets quite sloppy and disagreeable to get about on in places.

I am some distance—say one fourth of mile, and perhaps a little more—from the Capitol, but have a pavement and pleasant walk to the capitol-square, and my Committee room is on my way from my boarding house to the Capitol. Mr. Gretter and his family are very pleasant people, very attentive and polite, and free and easy

71. Kate was two years old at this time.

72. James A. Duncan was a distinguished Methodist minister and editor of the Richmond *Christian Advocate*. After the war he became president of Randolph-Macon College. Matthew Simpson, ed., *Cyclopedia of Methodism* (Philadelphia, 1881), 318.

in their manners, and I feel quite at home.[73] There are two members (one a Senator and one a Representative) of the Virginia Legislature boarding here, but all the family seems much more conversant and communicative to me than with the other boarders, but it may be because I have been with them a few days longer. My room is well furnished, large and roomy. Have a good bed and plenty of covering, and good coal fires. Every thing is quiet, and, alltogether, I am comfortably situated. There is not such a variety on the table as the hotels have, but there is plenty and nicely cooked.

We are getting on slowly with the business of Congress, and from present appearances will be here until March, if not longer. A resolution has been introduced in the Senate to adjourn the 20th inst, until the 10th of Jany. If it passes both houses I will telegraph you immediately to send for me to Lexington. I will go that way because the road is so bad to Abbeville. I may, however change my notion and go by Abbeville. I will telegraph you when and where to send for me. If it should so happen, when the wagon goes for me, that I do not get there at the time appointed, I want Bob[74] to try and get some hauling to do until I get there, and to wait at least *two days* for me. The rail roads often fail to make connections, and I may be behind time. Bob will, therefore, take along corn and fodder enough to do him four days—two to go and come, and two to stay.

I am glad to hear you are doing so well. You cannot imagine how anxious I am to see you and all my dear children. How glad I would be to be at home today. I do long to see Kate and hear her talk. And then, my dear Verdey. How much good it would do me to hear her say: "I want to kiss you." God bless my dear children, *all*. I have written all of them since I've been here, and hope to receive letters from them soon. Do tell them all to write me, and write *long letters*. Your letters are *very* short. Why dont you write more? Take a sheet, the size of this, and write a little every day between mails. Tell me every thing that is done—what the little children say and do—how the stable & crib are finished—whether my mules and corn etc are safe in them, how the mules look, how much milk the cow gives, how often you churn, how the wheat looks, is it thick enough, has Bob finished all the fence, can you get any land to cultivate next year? do the boys study? Who comes to see you, what cousin Sally says, who you receive letters from, what Judge Land wrote, etc etc. All these things are interesting to me. *Any thing* about home folks

73. This was the George Washington Gretter family, whose residence was at Fifth and Leigh Sts. Information obtained through the courtesy of the Confederate Museum from Miss Florence Gretter, of Richmond, Va., granddaughter of George Washington Gretter.

74. Bob was one of the Akin slaves.

and things, I will read with interest. When I received your first note I wrote you immediately and directed the letter to Abbeville, thinking that you might send there yesterday. I wrote on the back: "If not called for in two weeks, forward to Elberton." I did not know then when the mails would be open to Elberton, but suppose you have received from me several letters before this time and of course will not send to Abbeville. There was nothing in the letter as I did not have time to [remainder of letter missing].

Richmond Va.
Decr 14th 1864

MY DEAR WIFE: Yours of the 4th inst is just recd. and I am astonished at your receiving no letters from me. I know not what to think of it. I have written you five or six letters, one to Elbert & Warren and one to Eliza. I reached here late at night and wrote you the next day, and have written several times since. I would send you a dispatch now, but it has been ten days since your letter was written and you must have received several letters from me before this as you have had three mails since it was written. I have received three letters from you and they all will not make one of mine. I wrote you a letter day before yesterday of six pages, and have written you several long letters. I have written you every thing about my journey here, my boarding house, etc etc. and I feel sure you have my letters before now and will not repeat the same things. I am sorry to hear of the distress of poor Mrs. McTier. She is only one of thousands.

The resolution to adjourn as it passed the Senate, is only for eight days, and is only time for me to get home and return on the shortest rout[e], provided I make all connections,—allowing me to stay only one night at home. I cannot therefore think of going home and travelling eight days and nights, sleeping only one night. It may be amended in the House giving a longer time, and if I can have time enough to get home and stay a few days & return, I will certainly do so. You know not how anxious I am to go home.

I am a little fatigued this evening. I spoke nearly an hour to-day,[75] without finishing my remarks and have to conclude to-morrow morning, and wish to make some further preparation to-night.

What you wrote on the inside of the envelope of your last letter, was so torn in opening it, I can not tell what it is—yes, it is, you

75. The *Journal of the Confederate Congress* covering the proceedings of December 14 (VII, 356-57) does not indicate the subject of Akin's remarks, but two bills discussed at some length had to do with the sequestration of property of persons who had left the Confederacy to avoid military service and stabilization of the currency. Akin's speech probably was devoted to the currency bill, as inflation was one of his major concerns.

have no letter. I am sorry to hear it, but have received two mails since and I hope several letters from me. I expect to send this by hand to Augusta, and hope you will get it sooner by that. I wrote you the earliest hour I could after leaving Elbert at Abbeville. If I can get to go home I will telegraph you. Has Dr. Brannon [?] taken his things out of the room up stairs? I hope so.

I sowed two kinds of wheat. Have both kinds come up good. Bob can show you a stob marking the place between the two. Look at both. Has the fences been all fixed up?

You know not how anxious I am to see *all* my children, but more especially the younger ones. I do love John very much, and you know I love Verdy and Kate. I believe I want to see Kate more than any. And I want to see the baby too.

I am becoming *fond* of oysters. I find a good appetite recommends oysters very much. I have excellent beef, rice and sweet and Irish potatoes every day; but altogether I have a cheap boarding house so far as living is concerned, the price will be dear enough.

I have seen Feaster Woolley[76] & Emory Best several times since I've been here. Best has not yet had his case heard by the President. Feaster is still under arrest, and it is uncertain when he will be tried. Genl Wofford[77] is in Georgia, has been gone a month over his time, and it is uncertain when he will return, and, as he prefers the charges and is the only witness, no trial can be had in his absence.

Feaster says his father is very much outraged at Wofford's conduct towards him. Genl. Wofford has been to see his mother—and I hope has provided for her comfort. My dear, darling, do write me longer letters. I can get but two aweek and each one ought to be at least *four pages* of *large letter paper*,—six I prefer.

76. Feaster Wooley may have been Andrew F. Wooley who in 1861 and 1862 appears as a lieutenant on the muster rolls of Co. "F," 18th Ga. Regt. Emory F. Best, son of the Reverend Hezekiah Best, served as a major, lieutenant colonel, and colonel in the 23rd Ga. Regt. The cause and character of Wooley's difficulty could not be ascertained, but Best's arrest and removal from command, which occurred in June 1863, appear to have been influenced by dissatisfaction of his superiors with his performance at Chancellorsville on May 2, 1863, when most of his regiment was captured. See *War of Rebellion: A Compilation of the Official Records of the Union and Confederate* Armies (Washington, 1880-1901), Ser. 1, XXV, Pt. 1, 941 and XXVII, pt. 3, 918.

77. William Tatum Wofford, Cassville printer, newspaper publisher, politician, and a veteran of the Mexican War represented his county in the Convention of 1861 and voted against secession. After Georgia seceded he became colonel of the 18th Georgia Regiment. He was promoted to the rank of brigadier general on Jan. 19, 1863. He participated in most of the major battles in the East, was twice wounded, and was rated by Lee as one of his best brigadiers. He became commander of the Department of North Georgia on Jan. 20, 1865. He returned to Bartow County after the war, where he died on May 22, 1884. *DAB*, XX, 440-41.

Make each one of the children, Eliza, Elbert and Warren write to me every week.

God bless you and all my dear children.

Your devoted husband
Warren Akin

Save and turn all these envelopes. They are fine ones.

House of Representatives
Richmond Va.
Decr. 16th 1864

MY DEAR WIFE: Yours of the 8th inst. is just recd. It is impossible for me to account for your failing to receive my letters. I do not remember how many I have written you, but at least twice as many as I have received from you. I hope you received several letters the day after you wrote.

I wrote Elbert last night, and sent a letter off by hand to you yesterday, to be mailed at Augusta. I do not expect to close this in time to mail it to-day, but will do so to-morrow, and trust you will receive it before Christmas. Surely you have received my letters before this time. I believe I will send you a dispatch to-day, but when you will get it is quite uncertain. But I will send it to let you know that I am well. That is all I can say,—I have stopped writing, and have sent off a dispatch to you. You will not get it until Tuesday next, the 20th, but I send it now so that you may get then, and hope you will.

A speech is now being made in favor of appointing Commissioners to treat for peace. The resolutions were introduced by Turner of N. C. and he is now speaking, and denouncing the idea of putting negroes in the army. He is a great faultfinder, is an old Whig and denounces the democrats who were for secession and dont go into the army.[78] Turner has finished his speech, and Barksdale[79] of Miss. has offered a substitute for them, and the morning hour having expired the whole matter goes over until to-morrow, when we will have much gas and many words expended.

I have just been up to the Senate, which is in secret session, and heard several short speeches, in rather a conversational tone of voice.

78. Josiah Turner, disabled by wounds received at the battle of New Bern in March 1862, was elected to the Confederate Congress in the fall of 1863 on a wave of reaction against the Davis administration and the North Carolina Democrats who had capitalized on secession and war to push their old Whig rivals into the background. He was eccentric, captious, persistent and able, though in his long career in public life he was more effective as a critic than as a constructive statesman. *DAB*, XIX, 68-69.

79. Ethelbert Barksdale of Mississippi, member of the First and Second Confederate Congresses and a supporter of Davis.

There are about sixteen senators in attendance, and it is a very quiet body, indeed. This is the second time I have been in the Senate Chamber–once last session and to-day.

Governor Foot of Tenn.[80] is now speaking on the currency bill, and is rather *poking* Perkins in the ribs.[81] Foot does not pretend to argue the merits of the bill; but is simply replying to and criticising the remarks of others.

We are getting on very slowly. But one measure of importance has been disposed of by the House. A great many are pending, and have been partially discussed, but when they will be disposed of I can not even guess. I therefore think we will have a long session, and, as I have before stated, expect we will be here until March, and perhaps longer.

The hour of adjournment has arrived, and I will finish this at my room.

This evening Feaster Woolley came and staid until sundown, and I have had no time to write until now (night) and I have much writing to do. I believe I have omitted to tell you that I have to use candles, and tallow candles, too. The effect of writing so much is hurtful to my eyes, and I am burning the second candle of those I brought with me. Mr. Gretter told me yesterday that he thought he would have gas in my room to-morrow, and I hope he will.

I am sorry I cant go home Christmas, but must bear it as well as I can. The Senate agreed to a recess of only eight days, and the House refused that, So the matter, I presume, is at rest. The House passed a bill increasing the pay of the members fifty per cent but the Senate, I am informed, will not pass it, and no increase will be made. So it will take all the pay I get here, or very near it, to pay my expenses here. I will have to sell bonds or gold to get money to pay for my meat and corn. I have a hundred dollars in gold with me, and I can sell it for $3,400, but that will not be enough to pay what I will owe when I get home, as the corn pork and lard will cost about six thousand dollars, which would have cost a few years since $225.00. Two hundred dollars in gold would more than pay it. Had I not

---

80. Henry Stuart Foote, tempestuous, colorful and peripatetic politician who represented Tennessee in the First and Second Confederate Congresses until his departure from the Confederacy early in 1865. Before the war he lived in Virginia, Alabama, Texas and Mississippi. He served Mississippi as governor and U. S. Senator in the 1850's and the strong political and personal hostility that he developed for Jefferson Davis during that period was often manifested during his career in the Confederate Congress. He died in Nashville, Tennessee on May 20, 1880. Professor John Gonzalez of Mississippi Southern College has in preparation a study of Foote's career.

81. John Perkins, Jr., of Louisiana, was one of only 27 members of the Confederate Congress who served in all the sessions of that body.

better sell the gold? or what shall I do?— Please notice my safe occasionally. Notice the stable and crib doors and windows, and see if they are safe and secure. I wrote Elbert to have iron hinges made if necessary.

If you see Cousin Betsy Blackwell, or Mrs. Martin say to them I am wearing every day the coat and pants they gave me, and they are very comfortable in cold weather. A kiss for all my dear ones. Love to Cousin Sally.

Your fond & devoted husband
Warren Akin

Richmond Va.
Decr. 18th 1864.

MY DEAR WIFE: I commence to write you again, but I really have nothing to write of any sort of interest. I have written and written so often and having never received an answer to anything, it is discouraging indeed. And your last letter was so short—in fact telling me nothing about home scarcely. You say you borrowed Mrs. Thomas' barouche and went out to spend the day at Mr. Haire's, but you did not tell me whether you got there, who you saw, what you had to eat, what news you heard, whether Bob Latimer and his wife were there, why it was that George Latimer was behind so long, and nothing about the family.[82] Indeed, this is not right. Tell me every little thing. It will all be interesting to me.

Write to Mr. B. C. Wall[83] that you want to have the cow and ask when you must commence, and then have it hauled, and try and have a few shucks brought home on every load of corn.

Mr. Gilreath promised me to hire out Charles and Floyd for me, and I suppose he has done so before this.[84] Old man Prather is worthless, and I dont want either of my negroes to go there. If Bro. Gilreath does not hire them out, and you can do no better get Majr Jones to hire them for you to some one.

If you can get plenty of good shucks feed the mules on them. If you can not get shucks any where else send to Judge Herndon's to buy some. I was told that you could buy some good vinegar at a

82. Robert and George Latimer are listed in the 1860 census as the sons, aged 21 and 19, respectively, of William Latimer, a Cassville hotel keeper. Like the Akins, they apparently "refugeed" to Elberton to escape Sherman's forces.

83. B. C. Wall was an acquaintance with whom Akin had business relations. See letter of Wall to Mrs. Akin January 25, 1865 below.

84. Gilreath was possibly George H. Gilreath. Charles and Floyd were slaves of Akin.

Mrs. Hunt's some three or four miles from Elberton. You had better send there for it, as you may need it.

Do no letters come for me? Send me Judge Lands last letter. I have received a letter from Mr. Best.[85] He is at Dawson, Terrell Co. Ga. He says Bob. Best[86] has been back to his place in Cass, and that his house, fencing and every thing is burnt. Write to Mrs. Best. The people of Cass could all go home now. There are no Yankees there, But there are few houses, mills or any thing else left, and it will be difficult for them to live. Even the few that are there will find it difficult to get food and shelter I fear.

I am trying to live economically and wear my clothes longer than I do at home. I wear my flannels, drawers and night shirts two weeks, I have worn two shirts, all the past week—one three and the other four days. I wear socks a week. My handkerchiefs will get soiled, and I would wash them myself, but have no iron to iron them. A dollar a piece for washing socks and handkerchiefs is certainly very severe. Well, I cant help it. I do the best I can. I intend to save all I can because it is necessary in order to be able to live through the war. I do hope you will be able to get some land to cultivate next year. I must make some bread some way, if I can. Do the best you can in every thing, for it is very uncertain when I will be able to get home. I am so far from you, and it takes so long for a letter to reach me, you must act on your own judgment in every thing. I will write you about every thing I can think of and make every suggestion that occurs to me, but I cant think of every thing. Do have the cow well fed. I should regret if she should become poor. The little pigs, if well fed, may make good hogs in a year. Keep them in the lot all the time, & give them cooked food.

The loss of Generals at Franklin, in Hood's army was awful, thirteen Genls, six killed, six wounded, and one captured; and I have no doubt when we hear the truth our loss in officers of the line and of men was awful—far surpassing any thing in this war. We have a rumor that evening that Hood had another fight and has been terribly beaten, and I fear it is true. If so that whole army is lost I fear. Savannah has fallen before this, I fear, and if so I do not see how Charleston is longer to be defended.[87] If Savannah has fallen or should fall, (and I think it is almost inevitable) Charleston will fall, and then I fear B[r]anchville (the junction of the Charleston & Columbia roads) will be taken and communication with this place

85. Hezekiah Best, Cass County minister and planter.
86. Robert N. Best, son of Hezekiah Best.
87. The Confederates yielded Savannah to the Federals on December 21, 1864, and Charleston on February 18, 1865.

will then be cut off. If Hood can keep his army together, and take East Tenn. and take and keep possession of North Ga. & East Tenn, we will be compensated for the loss of Savannah & Charleston. But you will have heard all the news before this reaches you. I believe I have already written you that if the Constitutionalist[88] had c[e]ased to come to you to inclose a ten dollar note to the Editor and request him to send you the daily. Just write, Sir, Please send me the Daily Constitutionalist to this place. I inclose ten dollars to pay for it. Respectfully, and sign your name, Mrs. Warren Akin. Or request him to send the paper to me, just as you think best. I think, however, you had better have it sent as I have suggested to *you*, though it makes no difference to me.

I have just returned from church—heard an excellent sermon by Dr. Duncan. His church is the best lighted of any I was ever in. I think it has eighty six gas burners. You can see to read well in any part of the house. I heard Dr. Doggett[89] this morning. Both are excellent preachers, and I do love to hear them. This city is greatly blessed with good preachers.

I believe I have heretofore requested you to set Elbert and Warren to studying, and keep them at it as closely as possible. If the school opens send them, if no school make them study at home. Their time must not be lost, I am uneasy about them, and know not what to do. If I could make a good teacher, I would surely do it, but I can not and know not where to find one. I must therefore do the best I can. They understand enough in several studies to learn much by themselves, but with the aid you and Eliza can give them they can do much better. In nine months more Elbert will have to enter the militia service of the State, and O how sad my feelings are at the thought. But what can I do? Lord direct me! It is nearly ten oclock and I'll lie down and try to sleep.

God bless you my darling, and give you patience and resignation. Kiss all my children for me, and try and make the little ones understand it.

Your devoted husband
Warren Akin

---

88. The Augusta *Daily Constitutionalist* (1823-1877).

89. David Seth Doggett, Methodist minister and educator, prominent in Virginia before, during, and after the war. He was elected bishop in 1866 and died in Richmond on October 25, 1880. Matthew Simpson, ed., *Cyclopedia of Methodism*, 306.

House of Representatives,
Richmond Va.
Decr 21st 1864.

MY DEAR WIFE: Yours of the 11th & 12th inst. was received yesterday. It left Elberton on the morning of the 14th, and reached here on the night of the 19th and was therefore just five days on the road—and came in as short a time as it could. Your letters are generally eight days on the road, but if I can get this in the mail to-day, and it reaches you as soon as yours came, you will get it next Tuesday. But I fear it will not reach Elberton before friday, but hoping it will get through by tuesday I will write a short letter, while the business is going on. I have written you so many letters and told you every thing I can think of, I really have nothing to write of interest.

I obtained from Bro. Gilreath a promise to hire out Floyd & Charles for me, and I doubt not he has done so. Old man Prather is worthless, and I am unwilling to hire either negro to him without security, and for not less than fifty bushels of corn each, or thirty bushels of wheat each. If Bro. Gilreath should not hire them out, and should send them home ask Majr Jones to hire them out for me on the best terms he can.

I have written you, or rather, Elbert, about the money I gave him. You were right in giving the ten dollars.

I showed John's letter at table last night and had some laughter over it. Tell him to tell you what he wrote as I can not read it. God bless the little boy. Tell him he must learn to read so that he can read to me when I get home. Kiss and hug him for me.

Tell Mary I received her sweet little letter, and that I love her the "Crohonhotonthologusest" and the best too. Tell her she must be a good girl and write me another letter. Take her in your arms and tell her to hug you for me, and then write me what she says.

Tell Kate I am sorry I can not go home to see her. There will be no recess at Christmas, and I do not expect to get home until Congress adjourns, and I fear that will be March or April, and may be May. We are getting on slowly, and the great measures affecting the currency, taxation and the army, are still undisposed of. There is a proposition, now adopted, to dispose of the currency bill on friday. The tax bill has not yet been reported, and that will take a long time yet. I mean by "reported", that the Committee on Ways and Means, having the tax bill before them, have not reported back the scheme, agreed on by them, to the House. When that is done, the bill will be printed and made the special order for some day in January. When it comes up it will be read by sections, and each section will be passed on separately, and so will every amendment offered to each section, and there being so many members, entertaining different views, you see it will require much time, many days and perhaps weeks. The currency bill has been before the House over a week and will be two more days, and perhaps longer.

I have something to write you, but cant think of it now. If I think of it will write to night. I am at a good boarding house a quiet orderly place.

I wrote Eliza and Warren long letters a few days since, and had mail the letters before receiving his. I will write him in a few days again.

Give my love to cousin Sally Thomas, and tell her when I have *time* I will write to her.

Tell Elbert & Warren that I say they *must* study their usual studies and to get you and Eliza to aid them when necessary, and I request you to *make* them do it, at least two hours every day.

The House now adjourned, Good by, God bless you, darling

Warren Akin
House of Representatives

Richmond Va.
Decr. 22nd 1864.

MY DEAR WIFE: I wrote and mailed to you yesterday a hasty note, and sitting here this morning, (or rather this afternoon, for it is nearly two oclock) doing nothing, the House being in Committee of the Whole, on the currency bill, and Echols,[90] of Ga. is making a speech on it. What I meant by being in "Committee of the Whole" is this: The House resolves to go into Committee of the Whole on the Currency bill,—the Speaker calls to the Chair Mr. Clopton,[91] of Ala. and then any member of the House can speak, when he can get the floor, and can talk almost about any thing he pleases. The currency bill is now under consideration, and Echols is talking about having trust in God, and says God will send us a ray of light, and that soon—that God is with us, and we should be hopeful. He is making a very encouraging speech. He has just concluded, with these words, "The time will come when God will say to us: ye are my people and I have chosen you in the furnace of affliction."

Crisman[92] of Kentucky is now speaking,—we are still in committee-

90. Joseph H. Echols, member of Second Confederate Congress, from Georgia.

91. David Clopton, Confederate soldier and officer early in the war, and later member of the First and Second Confederate Congresses. After the war he served as Associate Justice of the Alabama Supreme Court. His second wife was the widow of Confederate Senator C. C. Clay. *DAB*, IV, 230.

92. James S. Chrisman, member of First and Second Confederate Congresses, from Kentucky.

but he is saying nothing about the currency bill, but talking about putting negroes in the army.

I have eaten but six of the sweet-cakes you put in my trunk. They are very good. On three nights, after sitting up late, I eat two. They are hard, but soften readily in water, and I enjoyed them, and I expect that I will have one of them when I start home unless I have to stay here longer than I expect. We have had *desert* but once at my boarding house, and that was plumb pudding and sauce, and you know I enjoyed it. O how glad I would be to eat dinner with you and my dear children Christmas. But it is out of the question to do this, and I must be patient and bear it. We do not have very rich eating at my boarding house, but I eat hearty dinners every day, but very little supper. I always become hungry before dinner, and eat heartily—generally too much. My bowels have been painfully affected, but are now entirely well. I enjoy remarkably good health.

Anderson,[93] from Ga. has just taken the floor, and commences like he intended to make a long speech. He is a good member, a moral man, a regular attendant at the Congressional prayer meeting. I like him very much, and also Mr. Shewmake.[94] They are both good members, and decent orderly men. Anderson is talking *good sense*, and *to the bill under consideration.*

The House will adjourn in fifteen minutes, and I will close this so that it will get in the mail to-day, and you *may* get this on friday the 30th inst.

The news from Hood's army is not flattering, and we feel a little discouraged, but hope for the best. I fear Savannah has fallen, and then Augusta & Charleston & Branchville will be endangered.

I have written you heretofore to send ten dollars to the Editor of the Constitutionalist, and ask him to send you the daily Constitutionalist.

Love to Cousin Sally. Kiss all my children for me.

Your devoted husband
Warren Akin

93. Clifford Anderson, member of the Second Confederate Congress, from Georgia.

94. John T. Shewmake, member of the Second Confederate Congress, from Georgia.

☆ 3 ☆

"Be As Cheerful As Possible"

Richmond Va.
Decr 23rd 1864

MY DEAR DARLING WIFE: If I could move with "the speed of thought" I would now be sitting by the fire with you and my dear children this cold night. The weather is very cold here now. A few days since and it was very warm for the season, even in Ga. It is now bitter cold. How many poor people are suffering to-night for food, fuel and clothing. How many of our soldiers are suffering to-night. O what anguish of mind and pain of body is caused by this cruel war! What suffering, grief, sorrow and tears are felt and shed all over our land. But the end is not yet. Widows will still be made, orphans will still be multiplied, anguish of heart still be felt and accumulating sorrows still roll over the hearts of fathers, mothers, wives and children. Blood will still flow and loved ones still suffer in prison. How long, O my Father, shall these sufferings continue? I suppose you have seen the letter of Mr. Howard describing the condition of Atlanta after the Yankees left it.[95] They even robbed the graves, and Atlanta is nearly ruined. I could not tell whether Solomon's house was destroyed from the description, as no names were given.

I have learned that many persons have gone back to our section of Georgia, and I fear have gone too soon, as I have no idea they will be permitted to stay there long. I think the Yankees will soon be in that country again. I have no idea of seeing where my house once stood until the war is over, if I do then. From all I can learn there must be great destitution in that section of Georgia. No hogs, cows, or sheep. How are the people to be fed? And then our own people are robbing and plundering the people who remained at home. There is a state of anarchy in all that section, and I fear will get worse every day.

From all I can learn I fear Hood's army is ruined, — scattered, and will never be good for any thing again. O what a disastrious cam-

95. The letter referred to is that of General W. P. Howard of the Georgia State Militia to Governor Joseph E. Brown, Dec. 7, 1864, published in the Macon *Daily Telegraph and Confederate*, Dec. 12, 1864. It is reproduced in full in Garrett, *Atlanta and its Environs*, I, 635-55.

paign into Tennessee this has been. I see Mobile is again threatened, Savannah I fear has fallen. Charleston will fall, then Augusta or Branchville, perhaps both, and then we will be in a right bad fix. An attack is expected daily on Wilmington, and that too will fall I fear. Blockade goods will then case [cease] to be used. Calico is selling here, I am informed, at $25. per yard, and soon will not be sold at any price. It seems to me we will soon be in as bad a fix as were our fathers in their revolution, when Charleston, Savannah and every other town of any importance was taken by the british. Clothes of all kinds will be scarce and high, and the most common necessaries will be difficult to obtain on any terms. No one can foresee the distress that will come upon the people in the next twelve months. Suffering must be extensive and severe. When this war is over many persons who had a handsome competency when the war began, will be in poverty if not in absolute want. I do not see how I am to continue to support my family. I never felt so before about it. I have some ten thousand dollars in interest bearing notes and at the present rate it will take the most of them—nearly all—to buy corn and pork for another year. I will either have to sell them or sell gold. Bartow County owes me nearly enough to pay for my corn and pork, but I cant get it. My expenses here for a few months, take all my pay for a year nearly. I do hope you will get some land to cultivate next year.

One more day and then it will be christmas. O how glad I would be if I could go home to-morrow.

Have you seen or heard from Col Price lately? What is he doing? I wrote to Mr. Gilreath to day that I had collected some money for him, and requested him to write me whether I should send it by express. If you can please write him a note & send it to "Broad River" Elbert county Ga." and tell him to write me whether to send his money by express. It is now late at night and I will stop and finish this to-morrow morning.

When you see Cousin Jane & Cousin Sally give them my love, and when you write do tell me every little thing about home and home folks. I wish I had something interesting to write you. I have promised to go out to the army Sunday if the day is pleasant. Good night my darling. How I do want to see you. Give my love to your mother and all of them when you write to them. Good night my dearest.

Saturday. Feaster Woolley has just informed me that he will leave here for Georgia monday morning, and I will not mail this, but will send it by him to Georgia and hope you will get it next friday, but fear you will not. I ought to have received a letter from you this morning, but got none, and I fear will not get any for some days to come. The weather is very cold and every thing out of order. Failing to receive a letter makes me feel anxious about home and causes a strong desire to hear from you. In the last week I have written and mailed two or three (the latter number I believe) letters to you, one to Eliza and one to Warren. It takes about three weeks for a letter to go from here to you and get an answer. So it will be about the middle of January before I will hear from you in reply to this.

Gold is selling here at fifty for one, or rather one dollar in gold will buy fifty in Confederate treasury notes. I think it will probably be higher in a few days. One hundred dollars will buy $5,000, in notes *now*, will buy six in a few days.

Savannah has fallen, Hood's army is nearly ruined, and I confess things look gloomy enough, but all will come out right some day. God rules on earth, and this war will work for the good of His people. And I will try to trust Him under all circumstances. "Trust in the Lord forever," – have patience, be hopeful, and try to be cheerful. When any one speaks discouragingly, you speak the reverse & try to cheer them up. *Talking* dispondingly will make one *feel* so. If you *feel* discouraged, dont express yourself so. Be as cheerful as possible.

A turkey sells for $125.00 here. I was offered this evening $300 for my gold chain, but did not sell. I was down on Main street a little while this evening and saw ducks, turkeys, partridges, a large buck, with 13 prongs on one of his horns, hanging at the doors of eating houses. I suppose many members will take their dinners at such houses monday. The house adjourned this afternoon until wednesday, so I have two rest days besides sunday. I wish I could be at home with you. I do want to see you "so bad." Do write me *long* letters. I have so much writing to do, or I would write more. My dearest darling do write me *long letters*. Your devoted husband,

Warren Akin

Richmond Va.
Decr 26th 1864

MY DEAR DARLING WIFE: I have no letter from you since the 12th, fourteen days ago, and I am anxious to hear from you.

I have written to W. W. Clayton,[96] of Augusta, to collect the in-

96. William W. Clayton, who became a prominent Atlanta business leader after the war, was at this time with the Atlanta agency of the Georgia Railroad and Banking Company. Before the fall of Atlanta, this agency and the funds in its care, including some Confederate notes deposited by Akin, were moved to Augusta. See Akin's letter to his wife of January 8, 1865, below and Garrett, *Atlanta and its Environs*, I, 712, *et passim*.

terest on the bonds & notes of mine I left with him, and to send you the interest. It will be some twelve or thirteen hundred dollars, and when you get it I wish you to pay Mr. Mattox[97] for the pork. I expect he will make you pay $1.50 per pound. Write him a note and request him to call and get his money. If he says you must pay him $750, ask him if he does not think the price is *very* high.

I requested Mr. Clayton to write you to Elberton when he sent forward the money to you by express, so that you may know when to send for it. When you know the money has been sent up to Lexington, get Majr Jones to see Mr. England, the mail carrier, to get him to bring the money over. You must write a note to Mr. Little, at Lexington depot, to send the money by Mr. England. Dont feel any hesitancy in attending to these things. All know that I am absent, and you have to attend to business for yourself. If when you pay Mattox for the pork, you have more money than you will have use for, to meet current expenses, pay Judge Herndon for the fodder I got from him. I am to pay him four dollars a hundred bundles. Elbert knows how many bundles he received. Elbert can pay the money. Judge Herndon is in Elberton every mail day. When you receive the fodder I am to get from Mr. Cleveland, pay him for it. I think I am to pay him four dollars a hundred pounds. Elbert and Warren are old enough to attend to such business and it is time they were at it. I can not live always and you and they will have to attend to these things when I am gone. I know you are not accustomed to it, but it is just as proper to buy meat and pay for it as it is to buy calico.

I went out to Anderson's Brigade[98] yesterday and spent the day. Had a good dinner. I preached for them. Rode out horse back and felt the effects of it last night. I was very tired, and did not get back until dark. The defenses are very strong, indeed, and I think the Yankees will be greatly slaughtered if they ever attack our men in their works.

I am writing in rather a cold room. The House has taken a recess to-day and to-morrow. I have been invited to two eggnog parties, but have not gone to any. I am going to see the Vice President.[99]

I wrote the foregoing at the House this morning. I went from there

97. Probably H. P. Mattox, listed in 1860 census as an Elbert County farmer.

98. Probably the brigade of General George Thomas Anderson in Field's Division of Longstreet's Corps. This officer was a Georgian, and his brigade was stationed near Richmond in the winter of 1864-1865.

99. Alexander H. Stephens, who early in 1864 returned to Richmond after an absence of eighteen months and resumed his duties as Vice President. E. Ramsay Richardson, *Little Aleck: A Life of Alexander H. Stephens* (Indianapolis, 1932), 272.

to see Mr. Stephens, he was not at home, and I have returned to my room and now am writing to my dear darling again. Since I have been in my room I have eaten two sweet cakes. They are very nice, and I am glad you put them up for me. O my darling how I do desire to be with you all to-day. It seems to me I never wanted to see my little children so much before. How sweet their words would fall on my ear now. And what is strange, it seems that I want to see Kate most of all. Bless the little thing. I would be so delighted to see her. But this may not be for a long time to come. I am sorry we are not discharging our duties to-day. But the members seem determined to have some time for going home and frolicking. I called for the yeas and nays on the motion for a recess, but one fifth of the members would not sustain the call. They did not want their names recorded on the Journal in favor of it, while they voted for it.

You can form no idea of the drunkenness here. One would think now that whiskey is five dollars a drink, that not much would be drunk, but the drinkers will have it; and when they pay so much for a drink, I am told they take a large one.

This is a damp, drizzly (is the word spelt right) day, and quite disagreeable, but it is very comfortable by a good fire. Being alone in my room makes me feel sad and lonely to-day and as I have nothing to do, and longing to be talking with you I write to you, while having nothing to write about. I wish I had something interesting to write you, but I have written you so often, I am run out of ideas and almost words, too.

It is reported here this morning that Foot, a member of the House, has gone to the Yankees.[100] I think this is not so, but he is gone toward the Potomac. He said before leaving that he was going to send his wife that way to Nashville, and that he was coming back and intended to go to Albermarle County in this State, and stay there. He said he did not intend to take his seat in the House again. If he does not most of the members will be glad of it. My seat was by his, but when he left he gave his seat to Mr. H. W. Bruce[101] of Ky. who is a nice man, and I am delighted with the change.

A few nights since the 12th of Octr. 1848,[102] came back to my mind with great force and pleasure, and O, how I did wish I could pass another night with the same feelings, the same joyous emotions I did that one. What ecstatic bliss it would be. Would you not like to

---

100. For a discussion of Foote's attempted getaway, apprehension, subsequent departure and expulsion by Congress, see Coulter, *Confederate States*, 135-36.

101. H. W. Bruce represented Kentucky in both the First and Second Confederate Congresses.

102. This was the date of Akin's marriage to Mary Verdery.

spend just such another night? The night after you receive this think of the 12th of October, 1848, and then write me the next day how you felt, – your feelings and thoughts. Tell me how you spent the christmas, who came to see you, who you went to see, what you had for christmas dinner, and how you enjoyed yourself. Tell me every little thing. Tell me all your troubles and trials. O, my dear, I want long letters. I sent off this morning, by Feaster Wolley, a long letter to you, one to John and one to Verdy. I think I have written at least a dozen letters to you and the children not yet answered. If I had answers to them now what a treat it would be.

It is not a great while before dinner, and after dinner I am going to visit some of my colleagues, if the weather be not too bad.

The health of the President is such he does not receive company, as I am informed. I want to go to see him, but do not know when I will have an opportunity to do so.

When you see cousin Jane and cousin Sally give them my love. As I cannot get this in the mail before to-morrow I will stop, and have perhaps some thing more to write before mailing it.

I have been to see Anderson and Shewmake, two of my colleagues, this afternoon. I dined there some time since. They are at a good boarding house, and very nicely and comfortably fixed. After leaving home Bell, Echols and Lester[103] called to see me, and I being absent they came on to see the gentlemen I had called on. I am now again in my room alone, and again longing for my "loved ones at home, "You see how large a letter I have written unto you." Contrast it with the *few words* I receive from you and perhaps you will "mend your ways." I hope so. But I fear you will conclude that my letters are words and nothing else. Well, be it so. Give me one of the same sort. I have to read your letters three or four times to make them long enough for one reading.

It is rumored that the President, Genls Lee, Longstreet and Johnson [*sic*] have had a conference, that Lee has been made Commanding General of the whole armies, and that Johnson has been placed in command of the Army of Tenn. with a *carte blanch*.[104] All I have heard speak of this, seem to be pleased. I do not know whether this is true or not. I am inclined to doubt it. Perhaps Lee has been placed in command of all the forces and Lee may have sent Johnson back to the

103. Hiram P. Bell, Joseph H. Echols, and George H. Lester were all Georgia colleagues of Akin in the Second Confederate Congress. The members from Georgia were exchanging Christmas calls.

104. The report was false but a move was under way among anti-Davis leaders in Congress to make Lee general-in-chief, and the hope was strong among those leaders that Lee would restore Joseph E. Johnston to command of the Army of Tennessee. The act providing for appointment of a general-

army of Tenn. If so I hope good will come of it.

I am surprised to find so many officers and men in favor of putting negroes in the army. This feeling is increasing rapidly, I am told, among the soldiers. I heard several say they thought it right to put the negroes in *now* and not wait until all the soldiers were killed.

I saw Jo. Headden yesterday. He said he had received a letter from his father dated in Novr. His father had been from home and reached Cassville just after the town was burnt. The Yankees gave Mrs. Headden fifteen minutes to move out her things, and as fast as she carried out any thing they wanted they took it and any thing they did not want, they broke it to pieces. Every house is burnt but four, Day's, Brown's, Jim Milner's old house and Mrs. Carter's. If this report be true, Chapman's & Mrs. Milhollin's houses are burnt.[105] What cruel brutes the Yankees are. How much like savages their conduct is. You doubtless remember hearing me say some time since—last year perhaps—that the Yankees would become more and more brutal and savage as the war progressed, and this opinion is being confirmed almost daily.

I believe I have never written you the hours of my meals. We eat breakfast about nine, dinner at 3½ and supper at seven, generally after that. It is now 7.25 and supper bell has not rang. I have very poor fare, but it must be so, or pay enormous price for board. I am trying to save all I can, and hence live hard. I was hungry one day at the House and bought one apple and paid one dollar for it. That was a costly apple, was it not?

Milk is selling here at ten dollars a quart—forty dollars a gallon. Only think of it! And nearly half water at that. Coffee is selling at thirty dollars a pound. Some one bought up all that was in the city, a few days since, at seventeen dollars a pound, and put the price up immediately at thirty. Butter has been selling at $12. a pound, but I have not inquired the price for some days. A partridge sells at five dollars at the eating houses. Only think of paying for a cup of coffee, a piece of bread and a partridge fifteen or twenty dollars.

---

in-chief was approved on January 23, 1865, and Davis on February 6, 1865, rejected a joint resolution of Congress requesting him to restore Johnston to command, but shortly afterward acceded to Lee's request that Johnston be allowed to report to him for an assignment. On Feb. 22, 1865, Lee placed Johnston in command of Confederate operations in the Carolinas. See Douglas Southall Freeman, *R. E. Lee* (4 vols. New York, 1932-35), III, 533-34 and IV, 4-5.

105. Mrs. Milhollin was the widow of Captain John F. Milhollin, who died from wounds received in Virginia while serving under General J. E. B. Stuart. According to Cunyus, *History of Bartow County*, 83, "Mrs. Milhollin with her 6 small children did not refugee in 1864 and at the time Cassville was burned found refuge at the fresh grave of her husband." The Chapmans could not be identified.

I see ducks, birds, and the finest mutton and venison hanging up at the doors of the eating houses. I have a notion to go to one some day and get dinner—have *one* good dinner while I am here. I have not had a *good* dinner in Richmond. Dont you think I ought to have *one*, at least? I do, and have a notion to take it. I expect it will cost at least $75.00—perhaps more. I used to get the finest kind of a dinner at fifty cents. I expect I write and read much more being here alone than I would if I had some of my colleagues boarding here. I must have something to employ my time, and when I [am] busy I do not have time to take the blues. You have no idea how I feel. Just imagine yourself away from home from *all* the children as well as from me for a month, and the prospect of being away two or three months longer, and you will then have some little idea how I feel. You ought to mail letters to me *three* times a week, Tuesday's wednesdays and fridays. A letter mailed wednesday will leave Elberton thursday morning. When you send it to the office tell the post Master to send it by Washington. Good night dearest.

"Calm [?] soothing sweet repose
On your peaceful pillows light,
Angel hands, your eyelids close,
Dream of Paradise to-night."

Tuesday morning, Decr. 27th

Again no letter came from you to-day. I am anxious to hear from you and my dear children. I know not why letters do not come from you. Do write me. It is damp, cloudy, gloomy this morning. No news of any importance. Kiss all my children for me.

Your devoted husband
Warren Akin

Richmond Va.
Decr. 27th 1864.

MY DEAR WIFE: I sent by Feaster Wolley yesterday a long letter to you to be mailed in Georgia, and this morning I mailed another long one (eight pages) to you, and now have commenced a third one for this week. Yesterday and to-day have been long days to me. Doing nothing and the weather cloudy, and the minds of many gloomy, and unable to hear from you all unite to make me feel unpleasant and disquieted. I went down town this morning and again subscribed for the Sentinel[106] for you. I hope you have sent for the Constitutionalist before this. While out this morning I thought my boot was leaking. On reaching home I took it off and found that there was a hole in

106. The Richmond *Sentinel* (1863-1866) was geenrally favorable to the President and was sometimes referred to as a Davis organ.

the toe of my sock. I took a needle and thread out of my trunk and darned up the hole and then put my sock on again. My boot was not leaking, but the outer sole has worn through, and I am asked forty-five dollars to half sole them, the price of five pair fine boots. Indeed that sum would once buy nine pair. I am almost out of the notion of buying Verdy a doll. Just the head, not as large as my fist, is priced at sixteen dollars. Flour is selling here at four hundred dollars a barrel. How much suffering there must be among the poor people. From what I hear this city must be very immoral. There are a great many women of ill fame here, and many who keep up appearances are not as good as they ought to be. Husbands and fathers are in the army, food difficult to obtain, temptation great and opportunity abundant, and the simple hearted go down to ruin. There is now a prospect of fair weather, and I hope it will clear off and remain so for some time at least. The gas works are out of order and the streets are not lighted at night, and I never go out at night. I have not been out at night, but once (except to church) since I have been here, and then I had two members of Congress to come home with me. I am afraid to walk the streets at night, and yet I am told the streets are full of women every night. A man, not long since, was knocked down in the street, killed and robbed, and I am a little suspicious about going out. But you need have no fears about me, I shall be prudent and cautious.

There are two letters on the way from you, that ought to have been received before this, and a third one that ought to be here in two days more. I know you have written me, if not sick, and if sick, I know some of the children would have written, and I try and content myself with the full belief that the fault is in the mail. And it may be that my letters do not reach you either. In order that you might hear from me, I sent you a dispatch which I suppose you received on the 20th inst. if not before. I supose you have received many letters from me before this time. How many have you received up to this day. I think I have received five from you, one from Eliza, and one from Elbert & Warren. When you receive this I want you to write me how many you and the children have received up to this day. This is your mail day. I want to see you so much, I almost wish some one would get sick so I would have to go home. I am almost sick to see you. You can form no idea how *anxious* I am to go home. And I am glad to inform you that others are anxious to go home too, for I begin to hear some talk of night sessions, and of meeting earlier in the day. I hope this will be done, and if it should be, then I may get home in February. I'm nearly crazy to go home. Well, I stop writing for the night unless I should conclude to have a little chat with you after supper. It is now six oclock P.M. and I suppose you all are now eating supper, or have just finished. Good sakes how I long to be with you! Write me what John, Mary and Kate say about me.

Wednesday morning Decr. 28th. Last night I went to see Dr. Doggett. He and his family are very pleasant people. His wife is a pleasant woman and so is his daughter. They have had, at different times, two children burnt to death. How terrible it must have been to their feelings. They live about sixty yards from where I board. I believe I wrote you some time ago that the old Doctor had called on me.

It rained last night again, and again it is dark and gloomy this morning. But the news from Wilmington is cheering, and helps out the bad weather.

After fire was made in my room this morning I went to sleep, the blinds were closed and when I waked up and looked at my watch it wanted a few minutes to nine oclock. Before I washed, the bell for breakfast rang. This is the only morning I've done so since leaving home. I will now stop writing until I go to the House, and perhaps, I'll hear from my darlings.

At the House

On arriving here I find no letter from home, and I feel a little uneasy about you and the children. But I hope nothing is the matter, and when christmas is over that letters will again come from you. I have nothing of any importance to write you. No news, a thin House, many members absent–gone to see their families–wish I could see mine–would be delighted even to *hear* from them. Do mail letters to me tuesday evening, wednesday evening and friday evening, and *make* some of the children write to me every time you do, so each one will write every week, and put their letters in the same envelope with yours and postage will be saved. What did Mary & Kate say to the letters I wrote them? I hope we will have new hours of meeting after to-day. If we can double the time now occupied in the House we we [*sic*] will certainly dispatch *more* business if it be not doubled, and we shall therefore shorten our stay here. The yeas and nays are now being taken on suspending the rules to take up a resolution to change the hour of meeting. The rules were not suspended, but I hope, on the call of the States a resolution will be introduced and passed for meeting earlier in the morning and for having night sessions, too. I am happy to state that a resolution has just been adopted to meet at 11 A.M. and take a recess from 3 P.M. until 8 P.M. and then adjourn at 10 P.M. This will make us work *six* instead of *three*. This will certainly hasten the day of adjournment.

Many members are opposed to night sessions. I am opposed to night sessions on one account, but I will have two members to go to my door with me every night.

Nothing more *now* darling,

Your devoted husband
Warren Akin

Richmond Va.
Decr 28th 1864

MY DEAR DARLING WIFE: I have mailed a letter to you to-day, one yesterday and sent one by Feaster Woolley to Augusta, (to be mailed there) on monday, and I am now writing the fourth one. But I have not one thing to write you. I believe I stated to-day that the House had adopted a resolution to meet at eleven oclock A.M. and adjourn at 3 P.M. meet again at 8 P.M. and adjourn at 10 P.M. This will give us six hours a day to work in, instead of three, and I think it will hasten a final adjournment of the session, which I very much desire. If you are failing to hear from me as I am from you, I know how you feel.

Let me suggest to you that you take a sheet of paper every night after you receive a mail and commence writing. Write all you think of then, before you stop. Next morning write again what occurs to you. After dinner do the same and after supper again write, telling me all the little sweet sayings of the children, and continue on in the same way, day and night until time to mail it. Then commence on another sheet and continue until the next time to mail a letter comes round. By this course you will write me many little interesting matters that you entirely forget when you write, and I will receive a letter long enough to do me some good. There are some things I would like to tell you, but fear to write them, and you will have to wait until I see you.

When I do go home I am inclined to go to Abbeville and go from there in the wagon home. This will save one day. But the road will be so bad I am almost deterred from trying it. What do you think of it? Write me your views. How do the mules look? Do have them well fed and curried, and try and keep them in good order. Have the cow well attended to, and dont let her get poor.

Be sure to purchase as many shucks as you can put in the stable loft, and have them pulled to pieces and feed the mules on them. If they do not eat them well, have them dampened with salt water. I suppose shucks can be purchased much cheaper than fodder, and the mules must have one or the other to eat.

I want you to make the boys get up every morning and take the keys and go and unlock the crib and stables. I do not want Bob to take the keys out while the boys are in bed. It is an easy matter for corn to be taken out of the crib and carried off before it is light in the morning. And I *specially* request that you will see that the keys are not taken out of your room until one of the boys takes them. Let no servant have them.

Have the cow kept in the old stable *every night*, and every day, too, when raining. Shelter from the cold and rain will prevent her from becoming poor, and will make her milk better.

Do your hens lay any eggs? Have you bought any more hens? How many have you? The hen house ought to be cleaned out and fixed up as well as you can, so as to raise as many chickens as possible. If you want more hens send out and buy them. The eggs they will lay will soon pay for the hens. And then the eggs are needed so often. Wheat is high and scarce, and with eggs you can make corn meal a most excellent substitute for flour. You ought to have fifteen or twenty hens, and two or three cocks will answer.

Have the rats disappeared any since I left home? Do they make as much noise as they did? How do your little kittens look? Do they catch any rats?

Have the plumb bushes growing among the strawberry vines dug up, and have the vines separated into rows. Be careful not to allow injured the pear tree near the corner of the square. It is a dwarf tree and will bear next year. There are some small cherry and apple trees in the garden that must not be injured. The young china trees in the garden must be dug up.

As soon as the ground is in good order I wish the lot below the garden and the one West plowed up—*turned over*, and the ground around Rachel's house and East of the horselot also. Have all the manure saved you can, as we will need all we can get for the garden and irish potatoes, and I am anxious to make as much as possible on the ground I have to cultivate. The garden needs much manure on it. The grape vines will need trimming, and those thick rows of currant [?] bushes will need trimming, so that both will yield as much fruit as possible. The trees, apple and peach, North of the garden & yard lot should be trimmed so that the ground then can be plowed and cultivated easily. Have all this done as soon as possible. I mention these things now because it is uncertain when I will get home, and I know you can't think of every thing at once. And if you have thought of all of them, I have done no harm.

The fence on the far side of the lot—on the back street needs some new rails on it, and the horse lot fence must be fixed up like the fence on the street. Well, my dear, here's another sheet full of words.

Richmond Va.
Decr. 29th 1864

MY DEAR WIFE: I mailed a letter to you to-day, but now commence another to my dear darling. I have read your letter three times. I know you must have enjoyed your visit to cousin Lou, and I suppose Mr. Walton's visit was pleasant and interesting to you, as you could ask him questions about our home neighbors and friends. How glad I would be to see him. When Cobb returns he will be able to tell much that is interesting. I wish I could see him.

Do not borrow cousin Sally's barouche too often. I know she will loan it cheerfully, but you might accidentally get it broke up and there will be no way of getting some of the materials to repair it. When I get home we will go visiting in our fine carriage—the wagon. By the way: just before tea tonight I heard a wagon passing the street and the rattling of the wheels was so much like mine I was about to go to the window to see if it was not, but second thought stopped me.

It has been snowing to-day, very slowly, most of the day, but melted as fast as it fell. The weather is very bad. To-day a resolution passed dispensing with night sessions. The weather is bad, the streets not lighted, some members not well, and danger of assassination in the streets, and, all things considered, it was thought best to meet at 11 oclock and adjourn at 4, sitting five hours, would be better than to have night sessions. And considering the probability of our frequently not having a quorum at night, especially when the weather is bad, I dont know but we will accomplish more by not having night sessions. And then, coming out of a warm room at night when the weather is freezing cold, one is so apt to be made sick. But I will get late dinner, – about half after four before commencing, and the sun will be down by the time I am done eating.

I told you to-day the articles of diet I had, and now say I have plenty of covering on my bed. When the weather is very cold I put my shawl over my feet. Most of the time I have to throw back some of the covering, as it is too heavy. The walls of my room are papered. It has two windows, with blinds outside and inside, and shades, too. The furniture in my room is all alike, chairs, table, washstand, bureau and bedstead all of the same color, – very similar to the furniture in the room we once occupied at the Trout House in Atlanta. I sleep on a feather bed, and perfer it in cold weather, especially as I sleep alone.

I am uneasy about Verdy and hope to receive a letter from you to-morrow telling me she is better. I trust you have not allowed her to remain sick long without sending for a physician. I wish I could see the little darling.

What does Price say about the conduct of his negro man? Does cousin Lu wish our scouts had killed him?

I am sorry for the people of Cassville. How much they must suffer. Poor old man Sylar and his wife, how I pity them. In their old age to be turned out of doors with every thing destroyed. I suppose all his tools are destroyed and the old man, therefore, has no means of doing any thing to make a living. I heard that Brown's and Days houses were not burnt, and I expect that Miss Brown & Mary Day saved them, from what I have heard.

If Benny [?] Houk[107] is a traitor I hope our scouts will hang him. Wonder if Sylar is still a union man? The Federal Union,[108] published at Milledgeville, says that the Yankee army made all the Union men good Southern men, and made "all the universalists in favor of hell-fire." I expect some of them felt like the yankees ought to be there.

I suppose the goods carried to Bartow by Cobb will be of great service to the people for doubtless many of them were in much need of them.

You have mentioned receiving but two letters from me, up to the 20th inst. I had written several letters before the one of the 14th. You must write me on the 11th of Jany and state how many letters you received from me written during christmas week. I sent off six pages by Feaster Woolley monday, mailed eight tuesday, six wednesday, six thursday, and am now on the 4th page for one to mail to-morrow, and I will mail one saturday, too, if nothing prevents, — Our pay has been increased fifty per cent. I get now six hundred and ninety dollars per month. This will pay expenses & I will have a little left to take home, but not enough to pay for corn and pork. And what am I to do along through the year? We will have to live poor— if we have bread and meat we must be content. Good night darling.

Dec. 29th House of Representatives

MY DEAR WIFE: I have just received yours of the 19th. Have you received but two letters from me? You do not write a word about any thing I have written. Nor do I know whether any of the

---

107. Possibly Benjamin H. Houk, listed in the 1860 census as a Cass County farmer.

108. This paper was known as the *Federal Union* until January 22, 1861; the *Southern Federal Union*, Jan. 29, 1861, to Sept. 16, 1862; and the *Confederate Union*, Sept. 23, 1862, to March 4, 1865.

children have received my letters, except the one to Eliza. When I write I expect something said in reply. I have sent off to you this week twenty pages written on paper of the size of this, and this is the fifth page I expect to mail to-day. Write me one six or eight page letter. Dont send such short notes. The few little words you write that Mary and Kate say are "sweet morsels" to me, why dont you tell me something more about the children, and home affairs. Every little thing about home will be interesting to me. If you would reply to my letters, in every respect, telling me how things are getting on. Your letter is very interesting, containing the news from our home folks, but it is so short, only three pages. O my darling, write me longer letters. I fear Col Price will regret going back to Cassville. The Yankees will be there again, I fear. I do not want Charles and Floyd to go back. But I suppose they are hired out long since, as Mr. Gilreath promised me to hire them out for me, and told me he did not want them next year. I have not time to notice what you have written more fully now.

Well, I have a large room, good bed, carpet on floor, a bureau, large mirror, rocking chair, good coal fires, and I use my boiler every night to get warm water. I cant get tricop[h]erous* to keep my head from itching, and I wash it with soap and warm water. This cleanses it and it does not itch. We live cheaply at my boarding house, yet I eat plenty. We have beef, pork, turnips, peas, beans, sometimes venison, mutton, chicken, goose, duck and turkey. We had several times dried mutton, broiled and buttered. We have butter at breakfast & supper, syrup at the latter meal, but sometimes no meat. Meat always at breakfast, – coffee & tea at both meals. I do not eat much except at dinner, but then I take plenty. I do not have to take soda often now, and my health is very good. I feel very well and have very little pain in my legs, and feel strong and *young*, and you cant imagine how *anxious* I am to see you. I have written you many things that I want some reply to.

When I go home to my room, & sit down alone and begin to think about home, I become very restless, and very anxious to go home. I know not how much I would give to see Kate, Mary & John for one hour. Do write me something *every day* & tell me everything the littles say about me, or any thing else they say. Every thing they say will be sweet to me. Make the children write to me. But pardon me for saying so much about writing. Any thing from home is interesting to me.

Love and a kiss to cousin Sally, and hug and kiss John, Mary & Kate

---

*A hair tonic. A young Charleston, S. C., businessman wrote in his diary, June 29, 1859: "Barber. 25. Tricopherus (Hair Tonic) .25."

for me, and kiss all my dear ones. If I could see fiddler now I would be glad and take him into my room to sleep. He would be company for me. Good by my dear, sweet darling. God bless you.

Your husband
Warren Akin

Richmond Va.
Decr. 30th 1864.

MY DEAR DARLING: This is the sixth letter I have commenced to you this week. One went monday by Feaster Woolley. Three have gone by mail, one to-day by Capt Dunlap Scott,[109] who will mail it at Lexington depot, and this I expect to send it by hand to-morrow. *Thirty two* pages of *words* have gone off to you this week, and how many will go in this I know not. Are you not mistaken when you sometimes say I dont talk to you? I'm sure I have held sweet converse with you every day this week, to a considerable extent. And, indeed, it is a sweet converse, darling, to sit down and thus speak to my dear wife, whose heart's best affections go out after me in all my labors, trials and troubles, – whose prayers follow me, whose love I know I have, one to whom I can with perfect safety, unbosom myself, and, whether in joy or sorrow, know she sympathizes with me, and with all my faults, love me still. Take it all together we have had a chequered life, and yet I think we have been as happy as most persons. Three of our little boys have died, filling our hearts with sadness and sorrow. I remember to-night the look of dear little Gussy when he turned his eyes to me when dying in pain, as if asking for help, and O the anguish of that moment! I could not help him! And I remember I never can forget it–when dear little Henry, struggling for breath asked me to sing him a song, and I well remember how he kneeled in your lap and kissed you fondly, seeming to say farewell. Would you not like to have a painting just as he looked with his arms around your neck, kissing you? What a picture it would be! The dying child kissing his mother farewell! These have been scenes of sorrow and sighing. But our little darlings, though absent from us, is not lost. They are happy and we may again see them–again live with them. God has honored us by making three of our children angels in heaven. They are in glory and we are invited to join them. Will we not do it? Will we have there all our children? O, my darling, you know not how much I pray for my boys. Will you not pray for them and talk to them about religion? Do my dear talk to each one of them on the subject. If Elbert would become religious,

109. Scott was Captain of Company "E," 8th Ga. Regt. At this time he was apparently on detached duty.

there would be no difficulty about Warren, I think. I wish you would try and see what you can do by talking to them on the subject.

It is growing late and I must close this.

I have sent by Capt Scott eight hundred dollars, to be sent to you from Athens by express. He will send it to Lexington depot to the care of Mr. Stokely, and you write to Mr. England to get it from Mr. Stokely and bring it to you, or write to Mr. Stokely, at "Crawford, Oglethorpe County, Georgia" to send it by Mr. England the mail carrier. Capt Scott will write to you when he sends the money.

I dined to-day with Judge Gholson.[110] He is a nice gentleman—a member of the House. Had a plain, but *good* dinner. I cannot write more now. This is a short letter and you must pardon me, this time, my darling, I "wont do so any more." "I didn't go to do it!" God bless my dear Verdy. Kiss all my children for me.

Make the boys study their books, if possible, and write about every thing.

Love and a kiss to cousin Sally.

Your fondly devoted husband.
Warren Akin

House Decr. 30th.

No letter came this morning from you. One you wrote on the 22nd ought to be here, and one of the 15th has not been received. I suppose they are on the way as well as one of the 26th, and another will leave for me to-morrow. I suppose from the number you have received from me, there must [be] a dozen or more on the way to you somewhere.

I do not expect to eat more than two meals a day hereafter while in Richmond. Taking dinner at 5 oclock, I will not want supper. Would it not be well for you to adopt the same rule? Have dinner, say at 3½ or 4 oclock, and then have no supper. The children would sleep better, and have, perhaps, better health. Think of this and decide as you think best, for you are the better judge of this matter.

Genl Wofford has just returned from Ga. He says every dwelling house in Manassas is burnt except Day's, Brown's, Mrs. Carter's and the Jim Milner old house.[111] My office, his office and all the houses.

110. Thomas S. Gholson was a Representative from Virginia in the Second Confederate Congress.

111. Akin was referring to Cassville and the destruction wrought there by Federal troops. After the armies passed on, the community was preyed upon by both Union and Confederate stragglers, by civilian maurauders and by irregular bands, ostensibly military and frequently Southern, whose loyalties were sufficiently flexible to enable them to plunder indiscriminately citizens of both Union and Confederate allegiance. For discussion of the activities of some of these brigands see T. Conn Bryan, *Confederate Georgia* (Athens, 1953), 148-54.

Mr. McReynold's house near the grave yard, is not burnt. All his mother's negroes have left her. He left a family of negroes there, and they, too are gone. Genl. W. says bands of robbers are going through the country and taking any thing they want and killing who they please. He told me two men who have been killed by our men. There is no law of any kind in that section. Genl W.'s family have gone back home. Old Mrs. Wofford was left alone for some months, without a servant or any one with her. Munford, Buford and Lowry [?] have gone back home.[112] I do not know how they will live. But I have heard corn was selling at $5 per bushel and meat at 25cts per pound, at Atlanta, and this would seem to indicate that provisions are more abundant in Elbert It may be that they have felt the weight of the tyrant's heel, and may feel more kind to the needy and distressed. There is corn on the Etowah River, in Cherokee county, but there is no way of hauling it. The horses are all gone, and nearly everything else, and the people are suffering much.

I am very sorry I could not spend christmas at home, but I am in the discharge of my duty and must try to be resigned and patient. God bless you, my dear, darling, and all my dear children. Love and a kiss to cousin Sally.

Your loving & devoted husband
Warren Akin

Richmond Va.
Jany 5th 1865

MY DEAR DARLING: I hope to receive a letter from you to-morrow, but fear I will not as the weather is bad and mails out of joint. I received a letter to-day from Col. Prather.[113] He is near Hardeeville, So. Ca. He has been recommended for promotion. I am going to see the President for him to-morrow. Old Wade[114] is doing Jack very mean and he says he will quit the service before he will serve under him, and I dont blame him. Jack says he hopes we will call the baby Susie, as it is the prettiest and sweetest name in the world.

112. Probably Lewis Munford, Alfred W. Buford, and Isaac Lowery, listed by the 1860 census respectively as farmer, Baptist minister, and merchant of Cassville. Lowery may have been Phillip L. C. Lowery, listed as a Cassville farmer. These men had apparently renewed residence in Cassville after a temporary exile following the Federal invasion. For sketches of Buford and Munford, see Cunyus, *History of Bartow County*, 51-52, 84-85.

113. Lt. Col. John S. "Jack" Prather who in the latter part of the war commanded the 8th Confederate Cavalry Regt., assigned to Wade Hampton's cavalry corps. See *O.R.*, ser. 1, XLIV, 934; XLVII, pt. 1, 1065. He married Mrs. Akin's sister.

114. Wade Hampton, renowned cavalry leader, planter, and statesman of South Carolina.

I had turkey for dinner to-day, and I ate two pieces breast and the meat off a side bone. We have sweet potatoes every day for dinner. And dinner is the only meal of any value to me. We eat breakfast about 9 A.M. and dinner a little after 4 P.M., tea between 7 & 8. So you perceive I have no chance to get to bed early.

I am more and more convinced every day that it will be March before I leave here, and perhaps later. We do get on very slowly. Yesterday and to-day nearly ten hours in all, debating two sections of a bill, and will probably not get through with the bill this week. Indeed we may not get through with it before the middle of next week. We have many very important measures before us, many of which will take a week to act on when taken up. There are so many many men, entertaining different views, it takes a long time to give expression to them. You must, therefore, make up your mind to be patient and do the best you can until I can get home. I fear Grant will run us out from here before April. I dont know how we are to recruit our armies, unless we put in our negroes. Jack is very much in favor of it. He says we ought to do it at once, and put in 250,000.

This is the only day in the last eleven that I have failed to send off a letter to you. I was so constantly engaged in the House to-day I could not write. It is now after ten oclock and I must go to bed and will finish this to-morrow. Good night dearest, Good night.

Friday morning. Jany 6th

My dearest, I received no letter from you this morning, and feel disappointed. I have been to see the President in favor of Jack, but could obtain no promise. We have so many officers and so *few* men it is difficult to obtain promotion unless there is a vacancy and then the person desiring promotion will have to be recommended *regularly* and come up from his superiors to the President. I do not know, therefore, what will be done.

I have been to see the Post Master Genl.[115] about sending mails to *our* section of Georgia, and he has assured me that he will do everything in his power to send mails to the people, and I hope we will soon be able to write to that country. I will send a letter to the Constitutionalist for publication on this subject, that the people may see what I have done and will be done by the Post Office Department.

I have been to see the President about organizing a force in our section to protect our people there against robbers and traitors, but do not know what will be done. He refers it to Genl Lee. By the way, I saw Genl Lee and had an introduction to him this morning.

115. John H. Reagan, of Texas, who competently filled the difficult position of Confederate Postmaster General throughout the war. See *DAB*, XV, 432-34.

He is, I think, a fine looking old gentleman, a pleasant man. I reckon I was prepared to form a good opinion, and that his distinguished service to the country had made a very favourable impression, and I was, therefore, in a condition to think well of him. I wish my children could see him. If we had peace and prosperity, as in former times, how glad I would be to have you and my children here with me. How happy I would be if you were all here today. O, my darling, how much I do want to see you and my dear children. But this cannot be and I will try to be content. If I could get three letters a week from you it would do much good to my heart. I have suggested to you the way of sending off three letters a week to me. Mail one tuesday evening, one wednesday evening (via Washington,) and one friday evening. I can write no more now. Love to cousin Sally, and a fond kiss to all my children.

Your devoted husband
Warren Akin

☆ 4 ☆

"I Had a Long Conversation With The President Yesterday"

Richmond Va.
Jany 7th 1865

MY DEAR LITTLE KATIE: I received your sweet little letter. I kissed it because my little darling had written it to her dear father. Do you love father now he is gone from you? Do you ever want to see father? Are you a good girl now? Now, my dear little Kate wont you kiss Mother for me? Put your arms around mother's neck and kiss her for father. You must hug and kiss Susie for father also. And kiss all your brothers and sisters for father.

Now, my dear little Kate, be a good girl and O how father will love you when he comes home.

Your fond father
Warren Akin

Richmond Va.
Jany 8th 1865

MY DEAR SWEET WIFE: Again no letter came from you today, and I am anxious to hear from you, indeed. I hope to receive a letter tomorrow from you. If I do not I fear I will become very impatient. You surely do not write me three times a-week, or I would get more letters from you. When I pass a week without hearing from you I become restless and anxious to know how you all are. I come to my room, sit down by the fire and my mind turns at once to my loved ones at home. I can see you all sitting around the fire and almost hear John saying something, and then I can see Warren enjoying it and hear you all laugh. I can see Kate's bright eyes and pretty curls, and I can hear my dear Verdy saying "I love you the best." And then I can see my sweet wife sitting there, too, with the children around her, looking thoughtful and feeling sad. And O how I do want to be at home. Here I am now, with a little table drawn up near the fire, with my boots off and slippers on, alone in my room, the family all gone to church, and I am here writing to you and thinking of you all and of the dreadful condition of the country. I have never expressed to you my fears of the future, but I am not able to see how this struggle is to end with safety to us. Instead of selling my gold, I think I had better sell my bonds and interesting bearing notes. I wish you at once to see Cousin Overton Tate and Mr. Bud Wall and know whether they will take the interesting bearing notes in payment of what I owe them for corn and pork.[116] Mr. Mattox also.[117] I expect they will refuse to take the notes at par, and if so, ask at what price they will take them? If they will take them at 80, 75, or 70 cents in the dollar I think you had better agree to let them have them and write to Mr. W. W. Clayton at Augusta and request him to send you enough notes to pay off all I owe. I will write to him at once to send the amount of notes you write for. The notes are selling here at about seventy five cents in the dollar. At this price it will take about $5,000. to pay what I owe the men whose names I have mentioned, and I will lose twelve or thirteen hundred dollars. But better lose this than all I've got. You can tell these men that I have the notes in Augusta and if they will take them you will write to Mr. Clayton for them. Tell them that it is not convenient for me to pay them in any other way. I suppose they will take them at the market value of the notes. *My opinion is* that I had better sell the notes at what I can get for them if those gentlemen refuse to take them. They will propose to wait until I get home, but tell them you want to pay them, and it is uncertain when I will get home. Get each one of them to say *how much in interest bearing notes it will take to pay him,* and then write to Mr. Clayton for enough to pay all of them. Have no unnecessary delicacy about this matter. Tell the gentlemen that it takes all my pay as a member of Congress to pay my expenses—that I can collect nothing that is owing me and I will be compelled to sell these notes to pay them, and that you want them to allow you as much as they can for them. Send for Mr. Wall and Mr. Mattox to come and see you, or go and see them. Cousin Overton the same, *and do this at once.* Of course you must not let any of the children see this letter. You know not how painful it is for me thus to write you, but my dear sweet darling it is proper, *important,* for this *to be done at once,* in my judgement. If you can not do this,

116. Overton Tate was probably U. O. Tate, the Elbert County farmer previously referred to. Bud Wall was B. C. Wall, also previously mentioned. Like many other Southerners who owed money at this time Akin was anxious to pay his debts before Confederate currency became entirely worthless. And like many to whom money was owed, Wall declined acceptance of the rapidly depreciating paper. See Wall's letter to Mrs. Akin of Jan. 25, 1865, below.

117. Probably H. P. Mattox, listed in the 1860 census as an Elbert County farmer.

write me *forthwith* for I wish to know on what to depend. I had the interesting bearing notes deposited with Mr. Clayton in the Agency of the Georgia Rail Road and Banking Company at Atlanta, for safe keeping and they were carried to Augusta with the funds of the Bank.

I am informed that there is a naval school near this place and that each member of Congress has the right to appoint a boy to it.[118] The boy appointed clothes himself & furnishes his own bed, but he is boarded by the Government and receives four hundred dollars a year. He takes the rank of a midshipman and is at once in the naval service. Would it not be well for me to appoint Elbert (he is now of the right age) and at once start him to school? He can get all his clothes from the government at government price, except shirts and drawers, and perhaps socks. It will cost me some five or six hundred dollars for his outfit, but he is not at school, and he must be sent to school somehow. After his education is completed he can resign his commission in the Navy or continue in the service as he sees fit. Think of this, consult Elbert about it and write me. I expect to do as you may wish in this matter. I do not know that there is any vacancy in my district, but will know in a few days—at least before I hear from you. If I have Elbert appointed he will have to come on here as soon as you can fix him up.—having made for him some shirts, drawers and socks, and pair of high quartered shoes, laced up before, neatly made and to fit well. All other clothes I can have made here in the Government shop. They will have to be made in the Naval style. Let your decision be made at once, and when made, it must be *final*. If he is appointed he *must come*. I can go home for him or meet him at Abbeville, or let him come here on the cars. He is plenty old to go any where. I fear you will think I am requiring a great deal of you, and, my dear, I know it is so. But I do not see how I could require less, under the circumstances. If I could so order every thing as to relieve you from the performance of any unpleasant duty, I should most certainly do it. But I can not do it; and it is our duty to make the most of our situation—do the best we can, be cheerful, try to be contented and resigned.

The meeting of the citizens in Savannah in favor of peace will have, I fear, a most unfavorable influence on the minds of the people. The news from Georgia is not good, but I hope better news soon. Gold sold here at auction yesterday at fifty for one, but it will go down I expect as it did a few days ago. It was up to fifty once before,

---

118. For a brief discussion of the Confederate Naval Academy, see Coulter, *Confederate States*, 299-300.

but fell to thirty seven very soon. But I am afraid to sell mine, as it may soon be worth a hundred. I must stop writing and go to bed as I have to get up soon and mend my socks to-morrow morning. Good night, dearest. *Keep this letter from the eyes of every one.* I will add a few words to-morrow. Good night.

Monday morning 9th Jany. Mrs. Mark Hardin is here trying to get her husband out of Fort Warren.[119] She sent for me this morning and I have just returned from the hotel where I have had a conversation with her. She seems much distressed—One of her children has died this year and so has her father, and the yankees took all her horses and mules and some of her negroes. We are busily engaged & have been for some days on a bill to consolidate the army. If the bill is passed, it will put muskets in the hands of many that now wear swords, and we need muskets.[120] No letter from you to-day. Well, I hope for two to-morrow. God bless you my darling is the prayer of your husband.

Warren Akin

House of Representatives
Richmond Va.
January 10th 1865

MY DEAR DARLING WIFE: I have just recd yours of the 1st inst. The one written a few days before has not been received. The letter just received is the only one received since the 26th inst. There must be three or four letters from you on the way here and I hope to receive them every day.

I regret my dear wife to see that your last letter is in such a complaining tone. It does no good to be unhappy. You had better laugh and be cheerful and try to be contented and happy. I cannot *now* write you fully in reply to your letter. I will write to-night and mail it to-morrow. I will mail this to-day.

You have never told me in any of your letters that Mr. Gilreath had not hired Floyd and Charles until the last one. He promised me to hire them out. I hope you have disposed of them before this. If

119. Mark A. Hardin of Kingston, Ga., a Confederate Cavalry captain, was captured on April 23, 1863, by Union naval personnel while attempting to run the blockade in a Southern blockade runner. He was confined at Ft. Warren, a war prison located in Boston harbor. Though steps looking to his exchange were initiated by the Union Navy on May 20, 1864, he was still in prison on March 23, 1865. See *O. R.*, ser. 2, VII, 153; VIII, 406-408.

120. Consolidation of depleted units, most of which had a surplus of officers, was authorized, but owing to tremendous opposition, from both officers and men fiercely loyal to their old organizations, the policy had only limited execution. See Bell Irvin Wiley, *The Life of Johnny Reb: Common Soldier of the Confederacy* (Indianapolis, 1943), 138-39.

you have not, when you receive this, write a note to Col. Thomas J. Bowman, and say to him I wish to hire out the negroes or dispose of them in some way. Take the 40 bushels corn for Floyd if you can do no better, provided the old man is prefectly good, or will pay the corn in advance, but he must shoe & clothe Floyd. Better let some good man take them for their food and clothing than to keep them at home doing nothing.

I regret you allowed Rachael[121] to have a dance, but hope no harm will be done by it. There will be no other occasion, I hope, to ask for another dance, but if it should be done, let suggest that it would perhaps be better to decline allowing it. If the children should desire to have a dance, I suppose you would hardly allow it, and they might think it very hard that the negroes should be allowed a privilege that was denied to them. But, of course, while I have my opinion, I can not undertake to direct you what course you should pursue. You must act, therefore, as you think best, and I will not complain. I trust, therefore, you will do *in every thing*, under *all* circumstances, just as your *judgement* dictates.

We are in secret session on an important measure, and I can not write as I wish now. I will write tonight. I have no idea when we will adjourn. I feel sure not before March,—perhaps a month later.

I am in much fear about the action of the Georgia Legislature that will meet soon. I fear a convention of the State will be called, and then *reconstruction* will, I fear, be proposed. If it takes place, no one can foresee what will be our condition in the future. I hear that meetings have been held in several counties in lower Georgia in favor of reconstruction, one in Thomas county, and Judge Lon Seward, and John R. Alexander in it and in favor of calling a convention.[122] Some counties have voted themselves out of the Confederacy and into the Union. There is a bill before the Congress of the U. S. providing for provisional governments in the rebellious states, and it provides that no person above the rank of Col. shall have a vote. What horror will follow re-construction. Its effects will be the same as subjugation, and horror of horrors will follow *that*. I have written you so much I will stop until I can look over your letter again. I am glad to hear the baby grows and is so smart. If I do not forget it I will take home some apples for Kate and Verdy. You would be

121. For Mrs. Akin's explanation of granting the servant Rachael permission to have the dance, see her letter to her husband of January 25, 1865, below.

122. Disaffection and peace sentiment became open and widely prevalent in many portions of Georgia early in 1865. See Bryan, *Confederate Georgia*, 153-55.

amazed to see the differences of opinions that exist among members. It seems, sometimes, that no proposition, however plain and simple, could be made that would not meet with opposition. I am much discouraged sometimes. Do write me cheering letters.

Your devoted husband
Warren Akin

Richmond Va.
Jany 10th 1865

MY DEAR WIFE: I wrote you to-day a short letter from the House and now write again. I suppose Mr. Hester saw Feaster Woolley in Augusta, and the letter was handed him then,—The letter you mailed to me on the 30th Decr, ought to have reached here five days ago. Yours of the 1st inst was mailed the 3rd and recd this morning.

I requested you in the letter I wrote this morning to write Col. Thomas J. Bowman, and request him to hire out Floyd and Charles for me. Say to him that Mr. Gilreath had promised to hire them out for me.[123] Indeed, he told me two men had spoken for them, and there would be no difficulty in hiring them out. I supposed they were hired out. If Cousin Overton Tate returns soon I think he will hire them out for you. Col. Bowman lives at Cousin Betsy Blackwell's. He is a clever man if there is one in the county. If he is not a *gentleman* there is none in the County. Do not trouble Majr Jones about any thing. He is like many other persons—money seems to be his polar star—and no wonder his children talk about, as of such importance, "plantation & negroes." If I do not forget it before sealing up this I will write a note to Col Bowman about hiring the negroes, and you will please send it to him if the negroes are not hired before you get this.—The people have become so selfish or this war is developing it, that the most of them seem unwilling to do any thing that dont *pay*.

I am glad you did not buy that old cupboard from Mills, and am glad he would not rent it, as I dont want it in the house. And I am gratified you can get along without it.

I am surprised at George Gilreath. He has acted very strangely. I have written him twice, but have received no answer. I requested in one of my letters with him a note, saying I had collected his money and request him to write me how to send it to him I can send it by express safely.

---

123. Floyd and Charles, Akin slaves, before mid-January were hired out, through the efforts of Gilreath—Floyd for 300 lbs. of pork and Charles for 200 lbs. See letter of Mrs. Akin to her husband January 15, 1865 below.

I wish you to tell Bob, *if he leaves the lot day or night, without your permission, I will certainly punish him if I live to get home.*[124] Keep this letter, and mark on it the day you tell him, and then keep an account of his going off, and give me this letter, and how often he has left without permission, after I return. Now, my dear, please do this for me. It may be unpleasant, but do it for me. I agree with you about Mrs. Brannon's [?] window curtains. I wish she would take them home, as they might accidentally get injured,–burnt or greased, and I should dislike it very much. I would be glad if she would take everything she has home. If she takes the table you had better have one made. Where is Joe Shackelford's husband? What sort of a wife has Bob Latimer? You have never mentioned her. Is Joe Shackelford's baby a girl or boy? What is the name?

I am sorry to hear you have the toothache. If I were at home I would try to cure it for you–I am sorry for Judge Land, but are you not glad his house is not burnt. I am truly glad. I believe I wrote you that Tom Word was living in it.

It is painful to hear of the people rejoicing at the death of the President. One regiment from Ga. the one that William was chaplain of, gave three cheers when they heard it.[125] I fear *greatly fear* the day is not far distant when those who so act now, will wish they had given the President a warm support, and thereby have prevented that which I fear will come, subjugation or reconstruction. The fate of the Confederacy will be settled in six months, one way or another, and I very much fear the *worst*. You can have no idea the state of things here. And amid all the gloominess of our prospects, there is much wickedness among the people.–officers and men, *in* position and *out*. Every one I converse with seems to feel that we are now passing a dreadful crisis, that will soon end in our ruin or in a brighter day for us. I fear Sherman will soon have Augusta or Branchville. When he gets to Augusta he will be in 70 or 80 miles of Elberton, and many negroes will run off and go to him, and he may make raids into Elbert to gather up negroes and horse. Grant made his negro troops drunk and made them charge upon our works a few miles

124. The slave, Bob, though usually a devoted servant while Akin was at home, was a recurrent source of concern while he was in Richmond. Many slaves in other parts of the South and especially in invaded areas, became haphazard in their work, resisted punishment or ran away. See Wiley, *Southern Negroes, 1861-1865*, pp. 51-52.

125. The identity of this regiment could not be ascertained. But it is a well-known fact that Davis's popularity, never very great after the first year of the conflict, sank to a very low level in the latter part of the conflict, both in the army and among civilians, and that many people openly denounced him. William is William M. Verdery, brother of Mrs. Akin.

from this place last fall, and they were slaughtered by hundreds![126] I had a long conversation with the President yesterday. He has been greatly wronged. He does not control the generals in the field. He did not send Hood to Tenn. He has been trying to get Genl Lee to accept the command of all our armies, but he declines. The President is not that stern, puffed up man he is represented to be. He was as polite, attentive and communicative to me as I could wish. He listened patiently to all I said and when he differed with me he would give his reasons for it. He was very cordial in his reception of me, and in his invitation to me to call again. And many gentlemen tell me the same thing as to his manner with them. His enemies have done him great injustice. He is a patriot and a good man, I think. He will have to do something more than any thing he has done before I can denounce him. He is the best man in the Government for his place. Many want him out of office. Were he removed to-day, we should be *ruined* in a few months, and I fear we shall be any way. Of course this is intended for *you alone*, I do not think I ought to conceal from *you* any thing. We are in a deplorable condition—standing on the verge of an abyss, the bottom of which no man can see. When we shall fall into it, or how to be saved from it, is hid from my eyes. I have not mentioned this to you before, hoping I would have some better news to write you. I trust you will *say nothing to any one* about what I have written on this page, about our future prospects. I wrote you some days since to try and pay for my corn, pork & lard with interesting bearing notes. If I do not use them in that way I fear they will be worthless to me. I was offered fifty for one to-day for gold, and I am told it is selling at sixty for one. I could not get an offer for bonds to-day at any price. Be sure to try and pay what I owe with the interest bearing notes *at once*. If Mr. Cobb brings or sends you any money for the county tell him you have no authority to receive it, and decline to take it. If he sends it to you by any one do not receive it. Tell him you have no authority to receive it. If, however, you can not pay what I owe with the interest bearing notes at *some price*, and Mr. Cobb should send or bring you any money and you can pay what I owe with it, take it and pay my debts. I fear you have received eight hundred dollars I sent you, and if you have, do not pay my debts with *that*, but keep it to buy what you may need. I fear

126. The reference is to the Battle of the Crater, near Petersburg, Virginia, on July 30, 1864, in which a Negro division participated, with heavy casualties. The charge that Negroes were made drunk before this and other fights was a common one, but without foundation. See Wiley, *Southern Negroes, 1861-1865*, pp. 329-41.

you have received it and used it as I have heretofore suggested, but hope you have not. You may pay for the fodder I bought of Judge Herndon and Mr. Cleveland. O, dear, my heart sickens at the trouble I am giving you. I wish I could go home. Please try to pay my debts with the interest bearing notes *immediately* and write me the result. I must pay my debts some way. I will try again to-morrow to sell a bond I have here, and may succeed, but fear I will not. I am tired, troubled, dispirited and will cease writing and try to go to sleep. So good night dearest, good night.

Wednesday morning, Jany 11th.

I had the pleasure of receiving this morning yours of the 4th, and am glad to hear you have hired out Floyd. I hope you will do something with Charles that will save the expense of feeding and clothing him. Do the best you can and I will be satisfied. You said nothing about receiving letters from me on friday, 30th ult and tuesday 4th inst. You ought to have received some letters by both mails. I suppose you were busy when you wrote and did not think about my letters. The letter you mailed the 30th ult has not yet been received. A long time on the way. Mrs. Hardin is still here, and seems much distressed about her husband. I feel sorry for her. I believe I wrote you she had lost her youngest child, born since Mark Hardin was a prisoner. Old Mrs. Hardin is dead. Took the small pox and died with it. Joe Hardin has separated from her husband and has been for two years. Mrs. Hardin is talking of going back to Bartow, but I advised her not to go, but have no idea what she will do. She leaves here to-morrow for her Mother's in So. Ca. and has effected nothing for the release of her husband. I was satisfied she would not when I first saw her. How many come here at great expense, inconvenience, trouble and hazard, with no chance of accomplishing any thing. Yet they hope. Eliza's letter was reced this morning with a few words in it written by you. Why don't you write longer letters to me? Take a large sheet, and not one of the *little* ones, or note paper. I am truly glad you get a little more pork for Floyd's hire. You will need it I presume before christmas next.

Do write me the sayings of the little children. They are interesting to me, very. Talk to them about me and tell me their sweet little sayings. I have a little cold to-day and do not feel as well as usual but am in my seat, attending to my duties. Write me often and long letters. I do not feel as *blue* as I did last night. The weather is now clear and bright, and I hope will remain so. Kiss all the children for me.

Your devoted husband
Warren Akin

Love to cousin Sally.

Richmond Va.
Jany 13th 1865

MY DEAR DARLING WIFE: I did not write you last night or the night previous, because I was too unwell. I was in bed all the day yesterday and until ten oclock this morning. I got up after drinking a cup of tea and went to the House, hoping to hear from you, but was disappointed again. Your letter mailed on the 6th ought to have been received this morning. I received a letter from Tom Hooper at Fort Delaware, dated 28th Decr.[127] He was quite well, but said he would give his left arm to be at home. He sent me a power of attorney to draw the pay due him, and to buy him a box of tobacco and send him. I bought fifty five pounds, at $7.00 a pound and it will leave for Fort Delaware to-morrow. There is a flag of truce boat now in the river. It brought about fifty thousand letters. The letter I received from Tom was brought by a returned prisoner.

Gov. Foot has been arrested at Fredericksburg, trying to get to Washington. He said he was going there to treat for peace. He has been absent from his seat in the House for some time.

Frank Blair was here yesterday from Washington City.[128] He came ostensibly to look for some private papers taken by some of our soldiers at his house near Washington. He called to see the President and inquired whether he would receive a Minister, Agent or Commissioner to treat for peace. The President replied "Yes, or I will send one if President Lincoln will receive him." Blair said that the Confederate States could dictate their own terms if they would go back to the Union. It is reported here that Genl Lee is in fine spirits and says "There is no cause for despondency–that we are in a better condition than we were a year ago." The people seem to be in better spirits than they were some days since.

I feel very well to-night. I had something like diarhea, and suffered very much. An old doctor, a member of the Va. Legislature boards here, and I sent down for him and he came up to see me two or three times. He gave me some dover powder three times, and I was relieved. O how I did wish to be at home. I was quite sick from the affect of the dovers powder. Did not get to sleep last night until after eleven oclock. Two gentlemen staid in the room with me until eleven. I dont think I'll be sick again.

---

127. Col. Thomas W. Hooper of the 21st Georgia Regt. was captured at the Battle of Winchester, Virginia, Sept. 19, 1864, and imprisoned at Fort Delaware. See *O. R.*, ser. 1, XLIII, pt. 1, p. 281.

128. For an account of the peace efforts of Francis P. Blair, Sr., which included two visits to Richmond in January, 1865, see Coulter, *Confederate States*, 551-52.

I wrote you a few days since to try and pay for the pork, lard and corn with the interest bearing notes I have in Augusta. When you learn from the gentlemen whether they will take them and on what terms, tell them you will have to send to Augusta for them and ask them if they will not wait until you can hear from me. Then write to Mr. Clayton to send you the notes, and write me at the same time what the gentlemen offer to take them at, and if I shall then think it is best not to sell them, I will telegraph you immediately what to do. I have better hope now than a few days since. A great deal depends on the course Georgia will pursue when the Legislature meets. I hope no foolish thing will be done.

My boots wore out very evenly on the bottom, and I have had a half sole tacked on without taking off the old one. This makes the bottoms thicker and my feet will be drier and less cold. We have had a beautiful day. It was pleasant almost like spring. And it is warm to-night for this latitude. I hope you will succeed in hiring Charles out. Do the best you can my darling and I will be satisfied.

Did you receive no letter from me on the 3rd inst. I have written many little things I would like some response to. You did not say how you sent Joe Shackelford to Ruckersville. Who were elected Judges of the Inferior Court in Elbert? Does Gilreath speak of going home? I am glad Majr Jones tried to hire Floyd. Why did you not try to hire Charles to that woman? I suppose you did. Why dont Warren write me?

Tell Verdy she must be a good girl, and that I say she must not cry. Try to make her understand how sorry I'll be to hear she cries so much. Dont scold her. Tell Kate I want to see her very much, and kiss both for me and try to make them understand it is for me. How glad I would be [to] see the little things to night. I hope Susie will be over her crying spells when I get home. I would like to see how she looks. You write me very little about the children. Write "a heap" of their sweet sayings. Write on the largest paper and fill the sheet. You dont know how often I read over your letters. Love to cousin Sally. Good night dearest, good night.

Saturday morning, Jany 14 [65]

My dearest darling, again I am disappointed in not receiving a letter from you. I am again in my seat this morning and we have up a very important bill and I write hurriedly. I have a bad inkstand, and have to hold the pen staff some distance from the pen, to keep ink off my fingers, and hence my bad and scattering writing.

I am very anxious to hear from you and will look to my letter box daily with much interest, and with anxiety, too, until I hear from you. One letter a week is rather a small allowance. Dont you think so? If your letters were like mine, six and eight pages, how much more interesting they would be to me. It would take so much more time to read them, and, consequently, I would feel *good* so much longer. I have so often urged you to write me long letters, that I am almost ashamed of myself. I pay $600 a month board. Every thing is very high here. I am doing what I never did at home. I wear but two shirts a week, and my drawers, flannels and night shirts two weeks, a pair of socks a week, and, therefore, have but a dozen pieces washed in two weeks. I carry and use my handkerchiefs until they are soiled so much, I am ashamed some times to use them. But I feel it necessary on account of the state of my finances. It is absolutely necessary to be as economical as possible, and I am practicing what I feel is necessary in this matter. My ink is bad and it is difficult to write at all. I have better ink now, and will write better. I have no news this morning. It is turning cold again. The House is now discussing the exemption bill, and that feature which exempts ministers of the Gospel. I have been at two sacramental meetings at Dr. Dogget's church. I have been to see him at his house & he came to see me first. He is a very pleasant old man, and his wife is a pleasant lady. His daughter is a nice girl. Well, I must close for I have nothing further to write. O, my dearest, may God make you cheerful and happy, patient and resigned. God bless you all my darling. I dont think I ever wanted to see you all more than now.

Good by darling. Love to cousin Sally.

Your devoted husband
Warren Akin

Richmond Va.
Jany 14th 1865

MY DEAR DARLING WIFE: I mailed to-day to you a letter. It is now night. I am in my room and have commenced writing you again. I can not write much to-night as I have my socks to mend, and it will take some time to do that. I have improved considerably in health and feel pretty well.—Well I have mended my socks. I used my ink-stand—the one I carry in my trunk—to darn on. It answers a good purpose. It is round and smooth, and I get along first rate. I wash my head in soap and water once a week. It keeps it from itching. In reading the bible to-night, I thought of you and all your troubles and trials, when I read "Cast thy burden upon the Lord and he shall sustain thee: he shall never suffer the righteous to be moved." O that you may be able to cast all your care upon Him, and feel that he careth for you. God bless you my dear darling. God bless you all. Good night, dearest, good night.

Sunday evening. On going to the House this morning hoping to receive a letter from you I was again disappointed. It is now eleven days since the date of your last letter. The one of the 29 or 30th has not been received. I try to feel patient and hope on, but I get very *anxious* to be at home sometimes. I had a delicious dream about you last night. I dreamed I was at home and you had your arms around me. When I waked up how sorry I was it was a dream. Is it not strange that things in dreams seem to be so real and produce such an effect on one? Nothing ever seemed more real in my waking hours than my dream last night. It is the first time I have dreamed about you since I left home. I have not, that I remember dreamed of home or any one there, and it seems strange that it is so, when I go to sleep thinking about you and wake up thinking about you. But I dream very little about any thing, and often dont sleep much. I wake up and roll over and over, but cant sleep. I am thinner than when I left home. The food I have to eat is nice & good, but it dont suit me like *home-victuals*. I would like to have home middling meat, corn field peas and corn bread, occasionally. My mouth waters while writing about them. And would it not be pleasant to have you comb my head this afternoon, and hold it and let me take a sweet little nap? O how sweet it would be. Well I can not enjoy these rich comforts today, but anticipation is worth something and I have a time looking forward to the hour when I will be at home. And O, my darling, I think we will be happier at home hereafter than ever before. Will we not honey? Wont we love and cherish each other more, know better how to appreciate each other, bear and forbear more readily and cheerfully than ever before, after our long separation? This morning fifty two days ago I left you—the longest time I have ever been from you. And is it not a long time? And then, the thought that I may be here a month longer, and, perhaps, a still longer time, comes up, and how dreadful it is. Do you love me, darling, any better when I am away than when I am at home? Does your desire to see me increase the longer I am away? Or do you become accustomed to my absence and feel it less? How is it with you? How long would I have to be away from you before you would cease to miss me? Think you that one year's time and separation would relieve you from the feeling which my absence now gives? If I was gone and you *knew* I would never return, dont you think your mind would cease to be troubled about me in a year? Would not the *habit* of acting for and relying on yourself soon relieve you from that trouble you now feel when you have to do these things? Dont you think if I were gone never to return that you would in one year cease to miss me? Would not the fact that you knew I would never return aid you materially in ceasing to study about me, and driving away from your mind those unpleasant feelings which my absence now produces? I have often told you that after I am dead you ought to marry again, but I feel so selfish about you this evening that I *now* have a *very* strong desire that you never marry any one when I am gone—unless you *know* him to be a better, wiser, and much richer man than I am. Then I will be willing; for then you and my children may be benefitted by it. And when I am dead and gone I want you to *remember this.* Well, now, dont this sort of writing to you seem foolish? And it may be; but remember that I am this bright and beautiful sabbath afternoon sitting by a good coal fire, alone in my room, talking to my dear, sweet, darling wife. She who has been so good to me, nursed me so tenderly, and watched me so fondly, and waited on me so unwaiveringly, with unremitting devotion day and night, without complaint, when pain of body, sorrow of heart, anguish of mind and trouble of spirit were felt so keenly by me. She, who, for more than sixteen years has tried so hard to anticipate all my wants, in food, and raiment, in short, *every thing*. She, who, when young and beautiful yielded me her hand and her heart, became my wife, the mother of my children, the idol of my heart, the sharer of my joys and the reliever of my sorrows. It is to *her* I write. And, precious one, I wish you could *know* this evening the full measure of my love for you. I wish you could *know* how much I desire to have you with me, and how delighted I would be could I have you and my dear children situated just as I would have you. Your every wish should be gratified, your every want anticipated. Nothing should ever mar your peace, disturb your serenity of mind, or shadow your pathway. Bright sunshine should smile along the way you go; sweet and many colored flowers should carpet the earth around you; the air should be redolent with their perfume; bright green foliage should ever clothe the trees and shrub about you; the song of birds, the noise of falling waters, and thousands of wind-harps should charm and lull you to sleep. Spring should ever bloom in all its freshness, and the sky, unclouded, should ever be spanned by God's bow of promise, telling of his kept faith and precious love to a sinful world. "Near a clear lake, margined with gold and whispering myrtles, glassing softest skies as cloudless, save with rare and roseate shadows, as I would have thy fate," should stand thy marble palace, as white as the "undriven snow." Thy pillow should be softest down. Angel hands should guard thee, and thy heart, ever blessed with the fullest assurance of faith and hope, feeling the constant presence and protection of God's unchanging love, should always rejoice, and "in every thing give thanks." And when the bright morning of a new & blissful existence was about to usher in upon you, angelic choirs, with harps, tuned by God's own fingers, should bear you away to His *own happy home!* All this would I give you, and more. But this would be enough. If after all our troubles and trials, we shall be permitted at last to gather, with our loved ones, around the throne of Him who made us, and redeemed us with His own blood, our pains and sufferings here, will, methink, be remembered only to heighten and intensify our joy and bliss in our new abode. Then let separation come, let trouble, and trial, and sorrow come, if God come with them they harm us not. *They* shall work together for *our* good. God grant that all our crosses and trials here may be a sanctified means of blessing us through time and eternity.

When the lovely morn is breaking
Gently o'er the sleeping sea;
When from sweetest slumber waking,
Mary, then, I'll think of thee.

When the evening shade is shedding
Balmy freshness o'er the lea;
When night's curtain round is spreading,
Mary, then, I'll think of thee.

When the Autumn leaf is falling,
Teaching man his destiny;
When the monster, Death, is calling,
Mary, then, I'll think of thee.

When this body cold is growing;
Verging on eternity;
When the web of life's undoing,
Mary, then, I'll think of thee.

And, when in yon heaven above,
When the Saviour I shall see;
And feast on smiles and purest love,
Still, methinks, I'll think of thee.

I inclose you a beautiful fragment, which I wish you to put in your scrap book. There is true philosophy in every line. Read it and think on it. Tell the children to read it, and try and memorise it.

If I spell any of my words wrong, please tell me of it, and then it will save me from committing the mistake again. I will stop writing now and close this to-morrow. You will not get it before the 24th inst. Lovely, precious one, good night.

Monday morning, Jany 16th.

This is a bright beautiful morning, warm and pleasant for the season, and I left my bed feeling unusually well and came here expecting to receive a letter from you, but am again disappointed. O the slow mails are so distressing when I fail to hear from my loved ones.

My darling, it seems to me that a few words from you would be *mighty sweet* to me, this morning. Do write me often, darling. I think I will be more satisfied, contented and happy, let will will happen. By the grace of God I intend to be resigned and patient under all circumstances. I intend to try and be more patient with my servants, children and my dear darling. If we could so far control ourselves, at all times, as to speak just what we ought, and, if we could act and speak at all times towards each other just like we did when first married, and before marriage, would it not be more happy? Would we not live a *sweet life? I intend to try it.* Let us both try it, and see if we do not find it an improvement. Well, darling, I'll close now. Good by—sweetest one.

Your devoted husband
Warren Akin

Love to cousin Sally

Richmond Va.
Jany 19th 1865

MY DEAR DARLING WIFE: I was engaged yesternight and this morning and did not write you, nor have I heard a word from you since yours of the 4th inst.—fifteen days since. I received a letter from Mr. Saxon to-day of the 4th and one from Mr. M Catchen of the 2nd from Covington. So you see that the mail came in last night, but none came from my dearest one. There are at least four letters of yours that ought to be here, besides the one of the 30th ult. What a treat these letters would be to me now. How I would love to spend two hours in reading and re-reading them to-night. And then I know they will have so many sweet sayings of little Kate, Verdy and John. O letters come on, come on, quick. But I can not speed them, and *must* wait until some slow mail brings them.

It is believed here that we will have peace soon. Many think that commissioners will be sent here by Lincoln or we will send commissioners to Washington. When Blair was here he asked President Davis if he would receive a Minister, Agent or Commissioner to negotiate for peace? The President replied: "Yes, or I will send one if I can be assured he will be received." Blair then urged the President to put in writing what he had said, and the President then addressed a note to Blair stating in writing what he had said verbally. When Blair left here he expressed the opinion that we would soon have peace. Returned prisoners say that the people of the U. S. are clamorous for peace, and that Lincoln will get no more troops at home, and it is known that he has ceased to receive any from Europe. The peace Democrat, Singleton, from Ill. was here, also, on a peace mission, but what he said is not yet known.[129] Much better feeling prevails here now than at some time back. The great fear *now* is that the people of Georgia will so encourage the Lincoln Government by their peace meetings that our present prospect for an early adjust of our difficulties by treaty will be blasted and we may have to fight another year.[130] If all our people should stand firm and show a unity of purpose and a determination to be free, it is believed the war will soon end. If negotiations for peace are once *formally* inaugurated, it is believed that the war will end soon thereafter. What a responsibility will rest on those peace croakers in Georgia, if they should prevent negotiations for peace and thereby prolong the war.

It is believed that the President will soon appoint Genl Lee commander of all our armies. This will restore confidence in the army and, it is thought, will be of great service in many respects.

It is also believed that General Johnson will soon be placed in command of the army of Tenn. His friends are clamorous for this. I am rather inclined to think it ought to be done. I have not much confidence in that army, and think it will have to continue to retreat, or, in military parlance, "fall back," and I think Johnson the best man we have for that sort of work.

If any one should inquire about the news from Richmond, you may read this portion of what I have written between the X.[131] Go over

---

129. James Washington Singleton, an Illinois Congressman of Southern antecedents, worked persistently for peace during the war. In the latter part of the conflict he made several trips to Richmond in the interest of peace. *DAB*, XVII, 191.

130. Leading Georgians interested in strengthening the Confederate cause, including Ben Hill and Howell Cobb, launched a speaking campaign early in 1865 to counteract the peace movement in their state. See Coulter, *Confederate States*, 554.

131. Akin placed one "X" in the margin at the beginning of paragraph 2 of this letter and another at the end of paragraph 4, thus, releasing for community consumption, paragraphs 2-4 inclusive.

to see Mrs. Dobbs and read it to the old man.[132] Gov. Foot has returned here, and made a speech in the House to-day, became so disorderly that he was finally forced to stop—He did not finish his speech, but said he would publish it, and I suppose will do so. If he does you may see it in the Sentinel. If not published in that paper and in some other I will send it to you.

Do you receive the Sentinel regularly? Do you get the Constitutionalist regularly? I have made many suggestions to you about many things, and suppose a great many of my letters have not been received, as you have made no reply to so many things. I think I have written you at least a hundred pages, yes, more than that, since I've been here. I sent you over forty one week. Considering the writing I have to do and the labours devolving upon me, I think I have been more attentive to you than you have to me. If you dont mend your ways, I fear I will have to scold a little. Now, come, do be a good, nice, sweet, charming darling as you are. Put in a few more sweet words to me in your short *notes*. Make "the old time come o'er me," when you wrote me from "Chieftains." Those were interesting days. You used to *answer* my letters, but dont now. Well, I'll write no more about this *now*, but if you do not improve I expect I'll have to give you a little love scold and see if *that* wont make you improve your manners. Well darling was up until near twelve last night, it is now after ten, and I have my bills to read and heat water and wash before going to bed. And as my sheet is full I must bid you good night, dearest, good night.

(2)

House of Representatives, Jany 20th 1865.

My dearest one: I came here early this morning hoping hoping to hear from you, but am again disappointed. What is the reason I do not hear from you? Where are your letters? Why do not they come to me? How often have I been disappointed on reaching the House and finding no letters! How *anxious* I am to hear from you, my darling. I do not think you know how I feel *now* when I cannot hear from you. Sixteen days, long days, have passed since the date of your last letter, and I know not whether you are sick, or what is the matter. I would leave for home but for the trust I have that the reason I do not hear from you is in the mails. This hope greatly relieves me, but it is only a paliative, and a very unsatisfactory one.

132. Possibly M. Dobbs, listed in the census of 1860 as a 75-year-old Cassville furniture maker.

Saxon wrote me for a passport to allow his wife and children to go to Nassau or Bermuda, and I have applied for it and will get it to-morrow.

MCatchin says the yankees did not burn any houses in Oxford or Covington as Sherman passed there. I think Genl Wofford will be assigned to duty in Northern Georgia. I saw the Secretary of War this morning and he recommended it.[133] Division Commander and Genl Lee had indorsed it previously. I think it will be allowed and he will go home, in a few days, and, if so I will try and write to you by him and you will then get it earlier.

Genl Foot returned here yesterday and made a long speech. He assaulted me (with words) with much severity, but said he did not intend his remarks as irony, yet every one (I know I did) believed he did speak ironically. After he ended his speech a resolution was introduced to expell him. You will see the proceedings in the paper.

I have just recd your letter of the 5th inst. It was put in Mr. Atkin's[134] box. This was one day later than the letter of the 4th received by me some time since. It is not necessary to inquire the price of tuition. If either teacher requires pay in provisions then it is out of my power to pay, and Eliza, in that event, will not go to school. Elbert and Warren had better go and I must take the chances of paying their tuition in some way. They *must* go to school, they *must* be educated in some way, and at every cost. This is my desire. It must be done if it so far diminishes my means as to render me unable to give them any thing else.

Whether it will be necessary to send Elbert or Warren with the wagon when Bob goes after any thing with the wagon, you must decide. As a *general* rule one of them should go, even if he has to leave to school. I hope you have had hauled up the corn & fodder before this time, and, if so, the wagon will not have to go off often. If the Yankees should take Augusta, or our troops should be in the county of Elbert, then the wagon should not be sent off without some one with it besides Bob. Our troops, as you know, are nearly as bad about taking horses as the Yankees. The mules must therefore be guarded as much as possible, for it would be difficult now to get a pair at *any price*. My mules would now sell at two or three times their cost. Hence their value to us and the importance of keeping

133. James A. Seddon was not officially succeeded by John C. Breckinridge as Secretary of War until Feb. 6, 1865, though he sent in his resignation on January 18, 1865. See Rembert W. Patrick, *Jefferson Davis and his Cabinet* (Chapel Hill, 1944), 57, 146. Akin's efforts were successful for, as previously noted, General Wofford was assigned to command of the Department of Northern Georgia on January 20, 1865.

134. John D. C. Atkins, colleague of Akin from Tennessee.

them. But the necessity of sending Elbert or Warren will depend on the circumstances surrounding you at the time,—the distance he has to go, is an important consideration, and the part of the county he has to go into.

I can write no more now. We are engaged in an important bill, and I will write you again to-night and will send it by Genl. Wofford, as I think he will go home.

My dear darling wife I am so anxious to see you. I wish I could go home. I know I would by the first train. Have no fears about me. Richmond will be in no danger for some months to come, and I will not be cut off from you until Columbia is taken, and I feel sure I will be with you before that time. If the Federals take Augusta mails will be sent from Abbeville or Anderson So. Ca. Good by dearest one. Kiss all my children for me. Love to cousin Sally. God bless you all.

Your devoted husband
Warren Akin

☆ 5 ☆

"Mr. Foot . . . Assailed Me Severely"

Richmond Va.
Jany 20th 1865

My Dear Precious Wife: I mailed to you to-day a long letter. I have just re-read yours of the 5th inst. and now writing to you again.

I have no apprehension of the Yankees going to Greenville, and think it unnecessary to write any thing about Liz.[135] I do not want her sold, nor do I want her sent to me unless it is necessary to keep her out of the hands of the Yankees. In that event I would like to have her. I would prefer her sold near her husband, if she could be sold without too great a sacrifice. Why do you mention this? Has your father or mother written you on the subject? If so you ought to have sent the letter to me.

I wish you to give Mrs. Dobbs every little attention in your power, (give her my respects and both the Mr. Dobbs also). She will need friends when confined, and may need some little things to eat that you may be able to furnish her. If so do not fail to do it. I would be glad if she knew my wishes on this subject. She is situated where the good wishes of any one may encourage and cheer her.

I regret to learn that you are alarmed about the condition of the country. I am truly sorry to know it. What good does your fears do you? They make you unhappy and tend to make the children so, and every one else you talk to. Away with your fears. Fear God and keep his commandments. Fear not man. We are in the hands of God, and if He is for us, what harm can befall us? Let us not suffer in anticipation. We will suffer enough when the time comes. It is wise to enjoy happiness by anticipation, but very unwise to waste our strength in rowing a boat before we get into it. Let us not labour before we enter the field, nor suffer from the rays of the sun before he has risen. It will be time enough to light the candle when the sun goes down, and let us not waste it by burning it while the sun shines, because we know it will be dark when the sun ceases to give light. Be of good courage,

135. Liz, a slave, was apparently hired out to someone in Greenville, Alabama, though she may have been staying (for her board) with Mrs. Akin's parents. Augustus N. Verdery and his family refugeed to Greenville, Alabama during the latter part of the war. Information provided by Miss Sally May Akin.

and God will strengthen thy heart. Let the words of the Psalmist be your words: "The Lord is my light and my salvation; whom shall I fear? The Lord is the strength of my life; of whom shall I be afraid? Though an host should encamp against me, my heart shall not fear; though war should rise against me, in this will I be confident." Try and bring yourself up to this faith. And let me beg you, my dearest one, to be cheerful. Be as happy as you can. Make the children as happy as you can. When you are in company, be as cheerful and lively as you can. When any one desponds, cheer them up. Tell them that if God is on our side, we will not fail; and if He is against us, we ought not to succeed. *I do not think we will fail.* I think we will succeed in some way, at some time. We may undergo long and severe trials, but I think the war is drawing to a close. You will see a short dispatch in the Sentinel to-day, from the New York *Times,* which says that Blair, Lincoln and Seward have been in "close consultation touching a proposition of Jefferson Davis in regard to commissioners for peace." If negotiation once *formally* commences, I think the war will end. And I trust we will soon have commissioners appointed on both sides that will end the war. If the Federals take Charleston, and I think they will, their pride will, in a great measure be satisfied, and then they will be in a better humor, and may more readily make peace with us.

You need not inquire, unless you desire it, what the price of tuition is. But I wish you to ascertain whether they teach only for provisions. If so, then tell Eliza to stay at home and study as well as she can, and practice her music as much as she can. If Harris receives his tuition fees in money, and charges extravagently high, then tell Eliza to stay at home. But the boys *must* go to school. Eliza is well educated compared to them. In all these things do what you think is right, my darling, and I will not complain.

You have not mentioned the receipt of any letter from me in either of your last letters. Surely some of my letters reached you on Tuesday the 3rd inst. and yet you say nothing about receiving any. Where do you get your paper you write on? I left plenty of good letter paper in both my trunks, and good envelopes too, but your letters are written on paper that I do not remember to have seen.

It is impossible, my darling, for me to say when I will get home. I hope to be with you in a few weeks—say four weeks—it may be six, or even longer. I will go home as soon as I can. But I can not leave here unless I have some good excuse. I have almost wished, sometimes that some of the family would get sick, so that I would have an excuse to go home. But a desire to see you is not considered altogether satisfactory. If it were I could obtain leave of absence at once, and would have been home before now. But I will have to stay here and suffer on and hope on. I feel now like I am nearly ready to leave here and go home wthout leave of absence. My dear darling you know not how *anxious* I am to see you.

As this will not leave here before sunday, and as I have two pair socks to darn, I will stop writing and go to work. Genl Wofford will take this to Augusta, and I expect you will receive it before the one I mailed to-day. Good night dearest, "All angels bless and guard you."

21st When I left my bed this morning I found it had been sleeting. The pavements were covered with ice, and I found it dangerous to walk, but I was very careful in walking and reached the House—walking very slowly through the rain,—without falling, or injury, to be again disappointed by failing to receive any letter from you. There must be several letters on the road somewhere. I hear no news from any quarter this morning. A resolution has been introduced to adjourn on the 24th inst, but it was laid on the table. I intend to offer one to adjourn on some day in Feby, but fear it will not be adopted. I know not what more to say. No news of any kind—no advice to give about home affairs, and having written so much to you about every thing, and receiving no answer to so many things already written, I know not how to write you. I was up until near twelve oclock last night darning my socks, and did not get through with one pair. The heels are now very thin and just ready to become a large hole, and I have been, and will continue to strengthen them so as to prevent a hole being made. I thus darned over one heel last night—a place nearly as large as the palm of my hand, and part of another heel, and expect to finish tonight. I have done such work several times, and will continue to do it as often as may be necessary. I can not wear socks with holes in them and will not hesitate to work at night to avoid it. I use tallow candles and they are trying on my eyes. The gentleman I am boarding with has been trying to have gas fixtures put up in my room, for some time, Yesterday a person commenced work and says he will have gas in the room to-day, I hope so, but doubt it. I have suffered for more than a week since I've been here, with an affection of the bowels, but my health is very good now, though I've lost some flesh. I think I am at least ten pounds lighter than when I came here. But I now enjoy very good health and spirits. While suffering for several days I was sometimes low-spirited and some thought I had the *blues*, but it was my health that made me sad, for I did feel sad sometimes, when viewing the condition of the country, and fearing I might be taken down sick here far away from home, or if I left for home I might be taken sick on the road, and then I could not have the attention of my dear wife, and who would wait on and nurse me?

"The touch of a gentle hand
Troubles can remove,
And pain will cease when lightly fanned
By the breath of love."

This is a poetical license, to a certain extent, but true to a certain extent. At least I do not want to be sick when I can not have the touch of my darlings gentle hand and be deprived of her loving kindness and tender care, and the fear of this made me feel sad. O, my precious one, how I love you and want to see you. But I must want on. This is a dreadful day. It is raining & freezing, and if it were a few degrees colder there would be a heavy and distructive sleet. As it is, the prospect is it will be very heavy. But I must stop. I send by mail two newspapers, one to Elbert & one to Warren.

My dear darling write me as often as you can. If any thing occurs requiring me to go home, telegraph me. Send the dispatch to Mr. H. H. Hickman, Augusta Ga. and request him to send it.

Your loving and devoted husband
Warren Akin

Love to cousin Sally.

Why dont the children write to me? Make them write. It will benefit their handwriting and composition, too. I was going to have my ambrotype or photograph taken today but the bad weather prevented it. 22. Genl Wofford has not called as he promised for this letter, and I fear it will be delayed longer than if it had been sent my mail. We have dreadful weather now. It is not very cold, but it is cloudy wet, muddy and *very* disagreeable. I went to hear Dr. Hoge[136] preach to-day. His text was 7 & 8th verses 54th chapter Isaiah. He did not come up to my expectation, but his sermon was a good one. His church is a *fancy* one. There are five windows in each side, the glass is coloured, and the five windows present all the colours of the rainbow. It is a singular looking house inside. It is not as large as many of the churches in the city, but is the most singular and *unique* one I have been in. Like the other churches it is warmed with heated air, and was uncomfortably warm to-day. The contrast on going in and coming out was very great. I received no letter from you to-day. Other members receive letters and papers, but I do not. It is terrible to me to go so long without hearing from you. I am becoming very impatient. There

136 Moses Drury Hoge, a leading Presbyterian minister of Richmond, Virginia, before, during and after the war. See E. C. Scott, compiler, *Ministerial Directory of the Presbyterian Church, U. S., 1861-1941* (Atlanta, 1950), 30.

are four letters of yours now past due here, and another due to-morrow, and another the next day; for I doubt not you write me three times a week.

Do you keep my letters? I wish you would. I had a dream about you last night. I thought I was lying down and you were lying at my back hugging me. O how good and pleasant it was; but it was only a dream. This is the second time I dreamed of you since I've been here. Do you ever dream of me? Tell me some of your dreams. Tell me *every thing*. O, my darling, what would I not give to be with you this evening! And how I do want to see the children, John, Verdy & Kate especially. One hour with you all would be worth a great deal to me. I am *so* tired being from home so long. But some of my colleagues have been away three weeks longer than I have. And some members have not seen their wives for two or three years. I do not know how they bear it. They surely do not love their wives as I do mine. I think I would lose my reason if I had to be away from you a year.

You will soon be fixing for gardening. I want a good many irish and sweet potatoes planted. Get seed some where.—If I can get there, I intend to go up to Cassville in May or June. And if we had any where to stay I would take you with me.—It is rumored that Mr. Seddon the Secretary of War has resigned, and that Genl Bragg has been appointed in his place.[137] While I think this a good appointment, so far as discharging the duties of the office goes, I fear it will not give satisfaction. It has become popular to abuse Bragg, and all the enemies of the President will denounce the appointment. It may not be true. You will see it in the papers, if true, before this reaches you. I do not know what to think of Wofford's not comming for this letter. Had I known he would have been delayed I would have sent the first part of this off two days since. Well, for the present, good by dearest.

Monday 23rd Jany. At the House

My dear darling, on reaching the House I found two letters from you, one dated the 9th and the other the 12th, the latter inclosing a short note from Warren. I think Warren's letter is decidedly the most laconic I have received.

Your long letter is the best treat I have received for a long time. O for a few more of the same kind. Genl Wofford has not yet called for my letter. If he does not call by the time I have to mail this I will let it go off by mail and write you again by him. Mr. Cobb writes

137. Bragg was not made Secretary of War, but continued to function as President Davis's principal military adviser, to which position he was appointed in 1864 after the defeat at Missionary Ridge forced his relinquishment of command of the Army of Tennessee.

me that he has fifteen hundred dollars to pay me. If he calls to pay you the money, receive it from him. I wrote you not to receive it, but now tell you to receive it and pay my debts with it. Take care of your money, and keep an account of all you spend, so that you will know when any is stolen from you. I received a letter from R. F. Akin (my cousin). He was at Union Springs Ala. Wants a favor done. How many letters I receive of this kind I receive, you have no idea of the labour I have to perform. I do my best for all. Mr. Cobb says his piano, two bureaus some beds and other things were saved for him. He says old Cassville is the most desolate place he ever saw. Not a house on his place is left. I will try and write to you to-night. Tell Charles if he does not do better I will sell him. Hire him if you can for something.

Blair is here again. It is rumoured thae he is accredited here to treat for peace. I do not believe it. It is also rumoured that he says we will be received back into the Union by giving up slavery. I should not be surprised if he does take this position and insist on it.

So no *more* darling. Kiss my dear children for me.

Your fond and devoted husband

Warren Akin

Richmond Va.

Jany 23rd 1865

MY DEAR SWEET PRECIOUS WIFE: You know how much I haue enjoyed your long letter of the 8th and yours of the 12th, which were received this morning. How long I was enjoying myself while reading them. If your writing was as much scattered as mine your eight pages would make at least twelve. God bless you darling for writing me so many sweet words. I'll kiss you for this long letter when I get home. Precious darling, I want to see you *now* worse than at any time since I left hime. Wish I could travel with the speed of thought, I would stay at home to night with my sweet darling.

I sent by Genl Wofford to-day, to be mailed at Augusta, a long letter, nearly twelve pages. He has gone to Northern Georgia to organize a force to protect the people there. I reckon his wife will rejoice when he gets home and will be near her all the time.

I have gas in my room now, and am writing by it. It will be a great relief to me. It is off at my side, now, therefore, the reflection from the white paper does not strike on my eyes. I know this will greatly benefit me. I saw J. B. Tippin here to-day. He promised me to call to see me this evening, but has not come. He may come after tea. I will stop and read again your sweet letters, and then notice such parts as require an answer.

Well I have read your letters. O what a feast! How I enjoy the reading of them. I want to see you so much I can hardly sit still.

Mr. Foot started to Washington, was arrested, came back, made a speech in the House, assailed me severely, then left the House again and says he will not return. A resolution to expell him was introduced and referred to a committee. He is still in this city.

A law has been passed to appoint a Genl. in chief, and Lee will be the man.

A great change is going in the public mind about putting negroes in the army. I have heard from different portions of Georgia, and the People are for it. I remember well the 25th day of December 1860. I remember how I felt when put in the large chair and rolled up before the fire. But my feelings then were not of the same kind they were the 12th of Octr '48. But I must not think of that night. I become too anxious to go home.

I have not tried to hire any one to mend my socks. I do not think the ladies here know how, and think they would not if they could. And then every one charges so high for every thing done. I save money by doing the work myself.

The women seen on the streets (most of them) are not what they ought to be. Poor witches, how degraded.

Do not my letters show that some of those written have not been received? I think you ought to have received more than sixteen.

Suppose you write me a half or whole page every night. Would not that be the better plan and then Sunday and Sunday-night you could write "a heap."

What is it darling you fear to write? Why do you fear to write it? Affairs of a public character I can not write and what takes place in secret session. But you have nothing of this sort.

When you want Bob to do any thing dont *ask* him, but *order* him. That is the only way to do Bob. *Make* him do just what you want— Well I think cousin Sally can well afford to loan you her barouche, after getting the use of my mules and wagon.

Genl Wofford's mother is old and he did not want to move her, and *all* her negroes had left her, and he carried his family back that they might be with his mother and is at home [*?*]. It is much cheaper living there than any where else in Georgia. Corn sells there at five dollars a bushel.

I am very uneasy about Elbert. He may have to go into the militia service next autumn, and may be killed or die. O how miserable it would make me. Do not be weary in well doing. Talk to him often. Talk to him alone. Tell him how much I pray for him, and how glad I would be if he had religion.

Tell Verdy the Yankees will not catch me, I think,–I intend to try and keep out of their way and will go home and see my dear sweet little Verdy. She must be a good girl and kiss Susie and Kate for her father, and not let Warren have the "spa [several letters illegible]" any more.

You ought to have whipped Charlotte, Charles & Allen, if they would not tell who mashed the kitten. You would then have reached the right one.

I wish you would make Lucy cook all the time, and then make Charlotte spin four cuts at least, if she has good cards, She ought to spin five cuts a day. That is what the negro women used to spin at my fathers, and the cook woman spun three cuts and did all the cooking. They spun ten cuts when the rolls were carded.

If you could get land enough to cultivate it might be well to keep Charles at home, but if you can not get land, hire him out at some price–better take his victuals and clothes than to keep him at home doing nothing.

There is no danger of the city being taken soon. Congress will leave here before the roads will allow the armies to move. An army cannot move like hauling a load of wood. They have so many wagons, cannon, and horses, a road at this season soon becomes impassable. Hence armies cannot move such weather as we now have. It will be April before the roads will be in a condition to allow a large army to move. I will be at home before then.

I believe I wrote you in a former letter that the resolution to adjourn was laid on the table. Congress will not adjourn before the first of March, if then. We do get on very slowly. We have so many talkers in the House, and so many things to talk about.

You ought to *make* Elbert and Warren get up in the morning and go out to see the stock fed. Tell them I *require* it of them. They are too old to be allowed such lazy habits. They must not longer continue in such a course. Tell Elbert I want him to have that decayed tooth pulled out. It must be out before I get home,–and *both* must get up in the morning and go to the lot and see the mules fed. How many new nails did Bob put on each pannel of the cross fence? Did he put any new rails on the back fence? Overton Tate said he wanted me to cut up, haul and burn the tops of the pines out of the bodies of which the rails were made. Have it done. Mix the pine with the oak and you will have good fires, and it will save the hauling of other and rich pine.

I will be glad if Mr. Loftin does teach school. He is an old teacher, and said to be a good one. If there is no school for boys, try and get

Mr. Lo[f]tin to direct Elbert and Warren and hear them recite two or three times a week.

Tippin has been to see me, is gone, and I must stop writing for the night. It is now after eleven oclock. I will try and finish this to-morrow and mail it. Good night dearest, good night.

Tuesday morning, Jany 24th. I ought to have received a letter from you this morning but did not. I received a long one from William, but have not read it. It is four pages, closely written. I will attend to him when I am done writing to you. I received a letter from Mrs. Frank Jackson to be sent by flag of truce. She is at Spartanburg. I have many letters to write now. One U. S. postage stamp is worth $1.50 in confederate money.

The President keeps a guard around his house because it is known that Yankees have tried to have him killed, and it is important to prevent this. A guard is posted around the capitol here day and night, to protect the house, records & papers. So are all the important public buildings. I stop now.

Your devoted husband
Warren Akin

Richmond Va.
Jany 24th 1865

MY DEAR WIFE:

The resolution for the expulsion of Henry S. Foote has just been acted on. It requires two thirds of all the members of the House to expell a member, and on the vote taken by yeas and nays, the vote stood yeas 51 nays 24. The yeas were more than two thirds of the members *present*, but there were 33 members absent, and fifty one is not even a *majority* of all the members of the House. How the members absent would have voted, no one can tell. If in the same ratio with those present, he would have been expelled. The House passed resolutions, one declaring that his arrest was proper, and the other that he deserved the censure of the House. The other day when I offered a resolution that his arrest was no breach of privilege, it was lost by one vote; and now the *whole house* declare his arrest was proper. If *proper* it was no breach of privilege, because a proper arrest can not be illegal. This is a sample of the proceedings of this House. The vote of censure was very large, only a few voting no. I suppose you will, perhaps, see the proceedings of the House, in the Sentinel.

I inclose you the resolutions adopted by the Legislature of Florida.[138] Show them to cousin Sally. She will see what the Legislature of Florida think of the President and of his course. She will, of course, differ with the members–Senators and Representatives–of the Legislature of Florida; and I would like to know what she thinks of that Legislature, and of the resolution. See her, and show her, *carelessly*, the resolutions, and then ask her what she thinks of them, and write me what she says. Tell me more about the views of the people you converse with–give me their words when you remember them.

I expect cousin Sally will marry a young man next time. It is very natural that she should–*provided* she *can*, and I suppose she will have a chance to marry some young gentleman of good appearance as her father is a man of wealth, and she has some property herself, and is a lively, sprightly little woman.

I mailed to you this morning a long letter, and will mail this to you to-morrow, and will continue to mail a letter to you every day, *if I can.* I may fail some days, and if you fail to hear from me, be not uneasy.

Mrs. Jackson sends her love to you and Eliza. She is near Spartanburg So. Ca. We are in secret session to-day, and I cant tell you what we are on.

Since coming to my room I have written several letters. There was no news in William's letter.[139] I recd two from Jack,–merely business notes.[140] I am more fatigued to-night than any night since I've been here and must take rest. So good night darling, good night.

---

138. The resolution was not found with the Akin papers, but it appears in *Florida Senate Journal*, Thirteenth Session (Tallahassee, 1864), 110. Adopted by both the Florida Senate and House on December 6, 1864, it stated: "Whereas, That in the re-election of Abraham Lincoln by the Northern people, they have pledged themselves to continue the war for the emancipation and arming our slaves against us—for the confiscation of our property—for the destruction of our homes—the murder of our citizens—the burning of our cities and the degradation of the white race and the exaltation of the black race,

Be it therefore resolved by the Senate and the House of Representatives of the State of Florida in General Assembly convened, 1st, That as all our sentiments and efforts towards peace have been spurned by the Northern people, as signs of weakness on our part, we cannot, consistently with our dignity and the interest of our cause, make peace propositions to them, but are, as we have ever been, anxious that this war should come to a close upon grounds securing our rights as a separate nationality.

2d. That we pledge our lives, our property and our sacred honor to our sister Confederate States to stand by them to the termination of the strife in resisting the army and government of the United Sates, and would prefer annihilation to reunion with them."

139. William was William M. Verdery, Mrs. Akin's brother.

140. Presumably Col. Jack Prather, Mrs. Akin's brother-in-law.

Jany 25th No letter from you this morning. Your long letter of the 30th ult. has not yet been received. I fear it is lost. I have no news, and am too busy to write more now. Nothing is known here encouraging or depressing. We have clear weather to-day, and it is very cold. I hope it will remain fair. I have a most ravenous appetite, and am nearly always hungry. I enjoy my food very much.

Good by darling
Your devoted
Warren Akin

January 25th 1865
Mrs. Warren Akin
MADAM:
Your note by Robert has been recd & contents noted as to the interest money on the $\frac{730}{\text{" } 100}$ I do not wish to take that at any rate as I have more on hand of that kind of money than I have any use for. I am taking of the new issue where persons are anxious to pay but I would prefer any good note of hand to the money Col Akin note would be more acceptable but please be not uneasy as I am not in want of any money whatever.

Respectfully yours
B. C. Wall

Richmond Va.
Jany 26th 1865

MY DEAR DARLING WIFE:
I received and read this morning with much pleasure yours of the 15th inst. I am now at my room and have just read your letter again. It is long and interesting, but I am disappointed in your failing to *answer* my letter of the 1st inst. I remember well that letter, and had hoped to receive a long sweet reply to it. How disappointed I am? O my darling, you ought not to do me so. If you had written me such a letter, I know I would have answered it without delay. I am glad to hear from Judge Land. I have written to him, but fear he will never receive my letter. I am glad he has sold some of his negroes. If he will, with the money received from them, buy a good home, I will be still more gratified. I am also glad to hear that Billy Chunn[141] was alive and safe.

141. Probably William Augustus Chunn, listed in 1860 as a 20-year-old Cassville lawyer. He must have been in the Confederate Army at this time.

Your brother William is unnecessarily gloomy. I am sorry to see it. But some people are never happy. I wrote him a long letter, and tried to induce him to trust in God more, and to try and believe that all things are for the best. But his reply did not manifest any improvement.

From what Eliza writes me I think you did right not to send her to school. She is sufficiently advanced to study and improve herself at home, and I want her to do this. But I have written you on the subject some days since. The boys must go to school at *any cost.* I have also expressed myself to you on this subject. I am surprised that you think I had rather you would not write to me about Elbert. This is a strange notion you have, and I am sorry to know you think so. You never made a greater mistake. I am greately troubled about him, and have been trying to know if I could get him in the Naval School at this place. If the militia of Georgia is kept in the service after September next, I do not see how he is to be kept out of the service. When he is seventeen, if the war continues, he will have to enter the service of the Confederate States. This thought is distressing to me. If he wrote a good hand I might get him employment somewhere. But he writes poorly and pays no attention to what I say about improving his handwriting. I am sorry for it. Poor boy! When I am dead and gone how he will regret his failure to take my advice. I wish he would do as I tell him, but he will not, and I expect nothing else than trouble from him as long as I live. He has mind enough to make a man, to do well, but I fear the worst. Let me beg you, my love, do try and get him to have his decayed tooth extracted. It is important that he should do so at once. Wright Carswell is absent without leave from his command, as I hear, and he may be arrested and sent back here.

As all our troops got away from Savannah, and no train of cars was captured by the Yankees between Augusta and Savannah, I do not see how Pleasant could have been captured. If he went to Savannah he certainly did not remain there after all the troops left. What was he going to Savannah for? I thought he had joined a company in Ala.

I am glad Floyd and Charles are both hired out. You get for their hire what would have brought in good money five years ago thirty dollars. But this is better than to keep them at home. I still want some land for Bob and Allen to cultivate. I want to plant about 15 acres in corn, and to sow about ten acres in oats. With a little aid in planting, Bob and Allen can cultivate this quantity and the garden etc at home without trouble. If I only get thirty bushels of corn, after paying the rent, it will be much better saved than lost. And the peas, fodder and shucks will be worth something. Peas will grow better on poor land than corn, and we will need peas for ourselves and our cow. If you can get any land to sow in oats, try and get cousin Overton to let you have seed oats to sow, and they must be sown in February, say by the 20th of that month. If you can get ground to plant in corn, then save some two bushels peas to plant. If you get land from cousin Overton, he will tell Bob when to sow the oats and plant the corn, and how to plant it.—Have you had hauled home the fodder I engaged from Mr. Cleveland? Better have it hauld.—My mules will need *roughness* next summer, and it will be difficult to buy fodder, and you had better buy *now* two or three loads of shucks.

Capt. Scott has returned here—was to see me last night. He says he wrote you and send the money from Antioch,—(which is seven miles from Lexington depot) between the 10th & 15th inst. There was no funds in Augusta to pay interest, and this, I presume, is the reason you have not heard from Mr. Clayton. When Scott left Augusta for this place Mr. Clayton had gone up the Georgia Railroad to hunt a place to move his family to. When he returns to Augusta and collects the interest due on my securities I suppose you will receive it.

One of my colleagues (Mr. Shewmake) will leave here sunday for Augusta to move his family from there to Lawrence County, and as this will reach you sooner by sending it by him than my mailing it here, I will send it by him to Augusta. I will also write by him to Mr. Clayton, and request the latter to send all my notes and bonds to you in the event Sherman marches on Augusta. And if you receive the notes and bonds you must not let any one know you have them—not even any of the children. I think I have in interest bearing notes $10,900.00 and in eight per cent bonds $6,050.00—in Georgia treasury notes five hundred and ten dollars making in all the sum of seventeen thousand four hundred and sixty dollars. It seems to me that I have more than this, but can not now recollect exactly how it is. I remember the amount of interest bearing notes, and State Treasury notes.

I do not now remember what it was I wanted to write you, but feared to risk it in a letter, but I feel sure it was something that ought not to be made public, and the mails are uncertain. Your letter written the 29th ult. is not yet recd by me.

It is singular that you were not invited to any of the social gatherings; but I do not think you were slighted. They have not the power to do *that*. You are too exalted to be reached by an effort of that kind, by any one in Elbert, even if it were purposely attempted. Never by any word or act of yours must you show that you thought it possible that such a thing was attempted, or *could* be, if attempted. By the way, who had dinings and teas? Did Mrs. Tate? Mrs. Heard? either of the Mrs. Jones? You must remember that very few persons in Elberton are old acquaintances of mine. There is no one in Elberton or immediately around there that I was acquainted with when I lived in the county except cousin Overton, and cousin Jane Jones and Judge Heard and Mr. Cleveland. I have been acquainted with Mr. and Mrs. Hester for several years, & Dr. & Majr. Jones also.

I am truly sorry for brother Glenn.[142] I wish I could see him. I would write to him if we had mail facilities. I am going to that county after I get home, if I can get there,—I saw the list of appointments for the Georgia Conference and looked for the name of Bro. Glenn, but did not see it. I saw the name of but one preacher sent up to that section, and have forgotten his name.

I am glad you dreamed about me. But who was it you were hunting and could not find in your dream? You must mind how you dream as I might become jealous.

I intend to try and obtain Genl Lee's autograph and take it to Georgia for the children. I expect Bro. Arbogast was about the only one that could be induced to take the presiding Eldership in our District, and he will not have many quarterly meetings to hold.[143] Mr. Cobb writes me that corn and wheat are plentiful in Bartow, and that he saw corn sold there at five dollars a bushel, and that there was more wheat in Bartow than in Franklin county. He says his wife has been sick for eight weeks, that his horse died the night before he was to start to Elbert to pay me some money, that his store was broken open and robbed of two thousand dollars worth of goods. If I do not forget it I will inclose a letter received by me from the Secretary of War, that you may have his autograph. His name is James A. Seddon. See if the children can make out the name. I will inclose herein a note which I wish you to copy on a whole sheet of the best note paper you have and put it in the best envelope and direct it as I do the copy, and without sealing send it to me and I will cause it to be delivered to him, and you may then receive an autograph note in reply.

I am sorry for John, but hope his hurt is not serious. Tell him he must not pick his nose, and must learn to read so that he can read the

---

142. Minutes of the Georgia Conference of the Methodist Church in the war years indicate that John Walker Glenn was presiding elder of the Rome District, which included Cassville, until the end of 1863 when he was superannuated at his request. Akin's statement suggests that Glenn may have tried unsuccessfully in 1864 to regain an active status.

143. Benjamin Arbogast, Georgia Methodist leader, served as President of the Cassville Female College in 1861-1862, as minister at Calhoun, Georgia, in 1863 and as presiding elder of the Rome district in 1864-1865. Information gleaned from various Methodist Conference Minutes by Willard E. Wight, who wrote a Ph.D. dissertation at Emory University on "Churches in the Confederacy."

papers to me when I get home. I did not sleep until after twelve last night and must close for this night. I hope the four letters you last received will yet be answered. I am anxious to see Susie. If I remember correctly, she will be three months old tomorrow. I do want to see Verdy, Kate and John so much. Didn't Warren laugh himself sick at John's "dot with a tail" and his "two dots." You ask what we are to do with Kate when I get home? Well, I suppose we will have to keep her between us at night. Is not the bed wide enough for that? I dont see what else we are to do, as she now sleeps with you, it will be a hard matter to get her to sleep by herself, and she will just sleep between us,—no other chance.

Good night my darling, good night.

Friday morning January 27th. I received no letter this morning. I have written to Mr. Clayton to send up my notes and bonds to you. Take care of them. I suppose you had better put them in the safe. You can unlock it and when you lock it again, pull the knob to the door to see it is locked. Put the bonds & notes in the vault inside the safe. The brass key unlocks the vault door. I have nothing new to write you. The Secretary of War condemns Glenn's conduct in breaking up the meeting in Jefferson county. I may write more to-night and to-morrow. I am writing in the House, and we are just going into secret session.

Saturday morning, Jany 28th. No letter this morning. I will send this to Augusta and hope you will get next friday.

This is the coldest weather I have felt in a long time. It is impossible to keep warm in this hall in such weather, without a better way of warming it. There are but two registers, both on the same side of the house, and the heated air does not warm my side of the Hall. I take off my overcoat when I come in the Hall but it is uncomfortable without it this morning. If you have such weather in Georgia I know you have a hard time of it. How the poor, half clad, hungry women and children must suffer this weather; and O how our poor soldiers must have suffered while out on picket duty last night. Many of them had their feet frost-bitten last night I fear. I learn that the mercury is 16 degrees below freezing point this morning and the James river is frozen over. We have had no weather any thing like as cold. I expect we will not stay in session long to-day.

I am greatly tempted to start home to-morrow. I want to see you all so much. I expect all my bonds and notes will be sent you by Mr. Clayton. Take care of them the best you can.

The House is now in session and I must stop writing. I send letters in one envelope to Eliza and Warren. If you will get the children to keep my letters, they will be highly prized by them long years after I am dead.

Kiss my dear children for me, and try and make the little ones understand it. God bless them all. God bless you my darling.

Your devoted husband
Warren Akin

P. S. I have just been informed that Blair returned here last night and left this morning and that Lincoln & Prest Davis have appointed commissioners to negotiate for peace. The President had a long conference with the Vice-President yesterday, and Mr. Stephens, Mr. Hunter of Va., and John A. Campbell of Ala. are appointed commissioners by President Davis.[144] I hope a peace may be made. If we fail to make peace the effort will have a good effect, for it will stop the peace clamourers in Georgia and elsewhere. But I hope for the best.

The House passed a bill to-day to put 40,000 negroes in the army as teamsters, cooks, pioneers etc. etc. This will put that many white men in the ranks with guns in their hands. This P. S. contains the best news I have been able to write you lately. Read it to cousin Sally and give her my love.

W. A.

[Inclosure: Letter
of January 26-28, 1865]

Confederate State of America
War Department
Richmond January 11 1865

Hon Warren Aiken
House of Reps.

SIR: I have the honor to inform you that the letter of Capt W. P. Milton relative to papers forwarded for appointment of field officers of the 30th Ga Regt. submitted by you, has been referred to the Adjt General for a report.

It will be impracticable to return the letter as desired by you until the report called for is received, as you will observe it was necessary to refer it for enquiry.

Very Respectfully
Your Odbt Servt
JAMES A SEDDON
Secretary of War

144. These commissioners met Lincoln and his Secretary of State, Seward, at Hampton Roads on February 3, 1865, but no peace agreement resulted. See Coulter, *Confederate States*, 551-53.

☆ 6 ☆

"I Must Stay Until I Vote On Some Important Bills"

Richmond Va.
Jany 30th 1865

MY DEAR DARLING. I mailed to you to-day a short letter, and started by hand yesterday, to be mailed at Augusta, a very long one, and being alone in my room tonight I must write you a few lines before going to bed. How happy I would be if you were here with me to-night. If we could move with the speed of thought I guess we would spend every night together. But this we cannot do, but I can in mind go to my darling. I can see you sitting by my little old table to-night writing, the little children are asleep, and you are thinking about me and writing to me. And now I can see you undress, put on your night gown and go to bed. I wish I was there. How slowly the time passes, – how restless and anxious I am to leave here, and how glad I will be when the day comes for me to start home. I think I will ask leave of absence after the 15th proximo. I will telegraph you a few days before I leave stating the day I will start and what day you must send for me. When you do send you must send a chair in the wagon, with corn enough to do the mules at least four days, for I may be detained on the road. If I should fail to meet the wagon at the time appointed, tell Bob he must try to get some hauling to do until I get there. He can go to hauling with certainty of hauling all day, for there is but one train a day for me to arrive on, and he will know, or can know, at what hour the train arrives there. I expect to go to Lexington and Bob can get the mules in a stable at Mr. Stokely's and Elbert and Warren can sleep in his house.

I suggested in the letter mailed to-day that you have enough blacking made to do a year, and that you have my thick heavy boots mended nicely for me. I will need them when I get home. You can probably buy enough lampblack from Mr. Hester at the tanyard. If not you can get it out of the chimney, or can make it by turning a pot bottom upwards and burning pine under it have one side raised to let the smoke escape and not have the blaze large enough to heat but hot enough to burn the soot. The latter is a good way to make it.

If you get it out of the chimney get it high up so that there will be no ashes in it.

Well, my dearest one, I will now stop for the night. Good night darling. Good night. All angels bless and guard you.

Tuesday, Jany 31st. My dearest one, I am again disappointed by failing to receive a letter from you. There are three letters of yours, or should be, on their way here, besides the one of the 30th ult. *that* I think will not come at all. I wish I had something to write you. But I have nothing of any sort. I received a few days since, a letter from my niece, Mary Young. She says that sister Jane's eyes are about the same. That sister Elizabeth has purchased corn at $2.50 per bushel, and pork at $1.25cts. per pound. I know not how she obtains money to buy provisions with. The poor have a hard time always; but at present their condition is terrible. The suffering for food, clothing, and in cities, for the want of fuel, is awful. Women and children are often seen on the streets begging for a little change to buy bread. I tell them to go to those who reside here. I know nothing about them or their *real* condition, and never give any thing, for the reason stated, and the further one, that I do not feel able to do it.–Gold has gone down here, and the brokers are refusing to buy. I hope the sending commissioners to negotiate a peace will have a good effect on the croakers and disaffected, and will restore, at least to a certain extent, confidence to the people. I am restless, anxious, tired, worried and feel like we are doing nothing as we ought. Congress seems not to realize the magnitude of the duties devolved upon it. I know not how to bring the members to think, "the ox knoweth his owner, and the ass his master's crib, but Israel doth not know, my people doth not *consider*." Here is the difficulty with the people and with Congress. They do *not consider. I wish they would.* You would be surprised to see how thin I am. I intend to weigh the first opportunity. I think I am fifteen pounds lighter than when I came here. I am going to-morrow to have my photograph taken, if the weather is suitable. I sold one gold dollar for sixty in currency and I am going to use it for photographs. I intend to have my photograph taken standing. I have been listening for a long time to Mr. Lyon[145] of Ala. on the tax bill and he is very dry, but the question is an important one and I have listened to him as well [remainder of letter missing.]

---

145. Francis S. Lyon, who represented Alabama in both the First and Second Confederate Congresses.

Richmond Va.
Jany 31st 1865

MY DEAR DARLING: This is the last day of January and I must write you a few lines, simply to be writing, for I have nothing to write you. I mailed you a letter to-day, but it was short and no news in it. It is reported that when a truce was granted for our peace commissioners to pass the Yankee lines, that there was a shout of applause all along both lines of battle–the yankees and our own. I expect the soldiers on both sides were really rejoiced to see that an effort was made to end this war. And O what joy there would be, from Maine to California, if peace should be made. May the Lord grant success to our efforts and send us a speedy peace. I suppose we may receive some news from Washington in about two weeks. It is barely possible that the peace Mission may keep me here a while longer than I expect. I hope it may. I will stay gladly if any thing good is accomplished. Mrs. Mosely and Miss Anna Gretter[146] have sent up to invite me to go with them to see a very pretty widow to-night, and, as you wrote me to go to visiting often, I intend to go. I have already fallen in love with that widow. She is a nice sweet looking woman. But I have seen her but once and was not long in her company then. Her brother I think is courting Miss Anna Gretter, and am inclined to think *that* is the reason for inviting me to go with them there. He will walk home with her to-night or I will be mistaken. I believe I wrote you the young widow's name was Mrs. Lane. Tell Eliza I got Miss Anna Gretter to hunt for the pieces of music she requested me to buy, but they can not be had in Richmond.

I am going to see the President again in a few days, if nothing prevents it. How many postage stamps have you? Count them and write me.

Again I find no letter this morning (Feby 1st.) from you. I came early to the House, went immediately to my letter box, and you know not how sadly disappointed I felt. But I soon was relieved by being told the House mail had not been brought up, and I hope yet to receive a letter from you. I went last night to see Mrs. Lane. She is a sweet, sad looking woman. She has one child. Her husband died the first year of the war, and she is now a clerk in one of the Departments, receiving as a compensation for her services four thousand dollars a year, or $333.33 a month. How she lives on it I know not. Flour has been selling here at one thousand dollars a barrel. It is lower now.

---

146. Anna Gretter was probably the daughter of Akin's landlady.

No letter, no letter from you this morning. Majr Henry[147] left Elberton about two weeks since, and says that you were well then. Why did you not write by him? I expect you did not know he was coming here. I am very anxious to hear from you, and intend to ask for leave of absence after 15th inst.–some time today.

I have just been to the hall of the House of Delegates of Va. to see a life-size portrait of Genl. Lee. He is standing looking at the enemy, with his arm resting on the end of a cannon, while his horse is held in his rear, a little to the right. I expect the Legislature of Va. will purchase the picture to put up in the State Capitol. The artist asks for it one thousand dollars in gold, or its value in Confederate money. The artist, I learn is deaf and dumb. The picture does not come up to my expectation, but it is good picture.[148] I wish the children could see the original. I would rejoice to have Elbert and Warren here for a week or two. I know they would be, not only interested, but much informed and instructed.

It is said that our Commissioners went on to Washington yesterday, through the enemies lines and that both armies raised a shout. I am much interested in what the Legislature of Georgia will do when it meets to-day-week, but hope nothing will be done to injure our cause and procrastinate the end of war and blood. The news I receive from Ga. is discouraging, *very*. I hope the rail road will be open to Atlanta by May, and, if so, I intend to go and see the ashes of our house, and the desolation the yankees have made at the old town. I have a bad cold–and suffer much, but I am quite well, otherwise, and feel like I could eat a good *big* piece of ham and a plate of cabbage, with corn bread, if I could [get] them. I have eaten ham only twice since I've been here. But I did enjoy it very much. When you send for me, be sure to send something for me to eat. I will be so glad when I get home, to eat with you and enjoy good ham again. What a treat a dinner of bacon and cabbage, or turnip greens, would be to me to-day. But there is no hope of getting it. [I am] hungry two thirds of the time. It is now one oclock and it will be three hours before dinner, and I am very hungry indeed. It seems to me I will never get used to the late dinner hour. I would like to eat dinner now and must eat something before dinner. We are again, today, in secret

147. This may have been David B. Henry who appears in muster rolls in 1861 and 1862 as captain of Co. "C", 35th Ga. Regt.

148. This portrait, painted by Edward Caledon Bruce of Winchester, Virginia, survived the war, and in the 1890's was in the possession of a New Yorker. Present location is not known. A discussion of the portrait, along with a reproduction of a sketch of Lee's face and shoulders, supposedly made by Bruce as a preliminary for the larger canvas, appears in Roy Meredith, *The Face of Robert E. Lee* (New York, 1947), 70-71.

session, but doing nothing of much importance. Every body is looking with great interest to the mission now gone to Washington. Different views are entertained by gentlemen as to the result. My fears are that it will result in re-construction, but hope I may be agreeably disappointed. No more now my darling. Good by. God bless you all.

Your devoted husband,
Warren Akin

Richmond Va.
Feby 4th 1865

MY DEAR WIFE: I sent you a dispatch by telegraph yesterday, saying I would be at Abbeville on thursday evening the 16th inst. and to send there that day for me. When Bob and the boys or one of them get there (dont send both boys) if I am not there I want them to stay there two days waiting for me. If I am not there by that time, then the wagon must return home. When Elbert gets to Abbeville, let him go to the post office and ask for a letter for him. If I am not there & he gets no letter from me, then let him go to the telegraph office and ask for a dispatch for him. It may be that I can not leave here at the time I have mentioned. If the road is not cut by the Yankees, and I can not leave here at the time stated, I will telegraph you the last of next week so that the wagon may not be sent for me. I have obtained leave of absence after the 11th inst. and expect to leave here on the twelfth, giving me ample time to get to Abbeville so that I will be there when the wagon reaches there. If I get there before thursday I will try and get to cousin's of mine on the road, which is some miles from Abbeville. If I cant do this, I will remain at Abbeville, so that the wagon may not be detained there. If the Yankees do not get to the Railroad, I may possibly have to go to Augusta, and in that event, Elbert will find either a letter or dispatch at Abbeville informing him what to do, so that he will not be detained. I have written to Mr. Clayton three times about my bonds and notes, but have not yet heard from him. Hope to do so in a few days. I am anxious to get my bonds etc. away from Augusta.

I have no news to write you. I will send this by hand, and will write another by another gentleman.

Hoping to see you soon, I am darling, your devoted husband

Warren Akin

Richmond Va.
Feby 5th 1865.

MY DEAR DARLING: I handed a letter yesterday to Wash Goldsmith to be mailed at Augusta for you. He said he would leave Richmond last night. I wrote another, similar to the one handed to Goldsmith, and handed it to a man who said he would leave Richmond this evening. Capt. Arnold told me to-day that he would start to Elberton to-morrow evening and I now write to send by him.

I sent you by telegraph on the ——[149] inst. a dispatch saying "send for me to Abbeville on thursday the 16th inst." I have obtained leave of absence after the 11th, and expect to leave here at night on the eleventh or the next day. I directed you to send for me to Abbeville because I feared the road at Branchville would be cut before I could leave here. I have written to Mr. Clayton to send you all my bonds and notes. There 109 hundred dollar interest bearing notes, making ten thousand and nine hundred dollars; and over six thousand dollars of eight per cent bonds, and five hundred and ten dollars in Georgia Treasury notes. I expect you had better not pay any of my debts until I get home. I obtained leave of absence to go to Augusta to look after my interest after the eleventh inst. with a promise that if it was not necessary for me to go I should not do so. I may not, therefore, leave here at the time mentioned. If I do not and the wires are not cut between this and Augusta, I will telegraph you in time not to send for me. If you fail to receive a dispatch from me on tuesday the 14th you may send for me with the hope of my being at Abbeville when the wagon gets there. If when Elbert gets there he does not find me, he must go to the post office and inquire for a letter for him (Elbert Akin) and if I am not on my way he will find a letter from me telling him what to do. If he receives no letter from me then the wagon will remain and try and get some hauling to do, and if I do not get there the next evening he must go again to the post office as soon as the mail is open and inquire for a letter for him. If he still receives no letter, he will wait another day, and still haul, and if I am not there the second day and he gets no letter saying what he must do, he will then return home. It will be sunday then when he gets home. If he does not, therefore, return home friday the 17th you need not feel uneasy. And if he should not reach home even on sunday the 19th you need not feel uneasy as Elbert may receive a letter from me telling him to stay until I get there. The travel on the road is slow and uncertain and I may be detained

149. Akin left blank the space for the date of the telegram.

on the road. If I am, I will send you a dispatch to Columbia, to be sent from there to Abbeville to Elbert.

I have had cold for a week and am suffering with it considerably. And the gas is impure and the odor from it is very disagreeable, indeed, and affects the mucous membrane of nostrils very much.

I went yesterday evening out to see Woffords Brigade. Major Bird (the Q. M. of the Brigade) sent an ambulance for me and I went out and staid with him. He is a son of old Elijah Bird of Polk. He is married. His wife is in Floriday. He had a hard bed. He is in a house (cabbin of logs) with a floor and brick chimney. He had a good supper and breakfast. I preached to the Brigade to-day in the wind and sunshine. Genl DuBose[150] is in command of the Brigade now. He is Genl Toombs soninlaw. I dined with him. He is very much of a gentlemen, and does not seem to be puffed up with promotion. I like him very much.

On returning to Richmond this evening I found our commissioners (Stephens, Hunter, & Campbell) had returned. They met Lincoln and Seward at Old Point. They were asked what proposition they had to offer. Our commissioners replied: "Independence and recognition." Lincoln told them he would not listen to such a thing and could only refer them to his proclamation. It is reported (but I do not believe it) that Mr. Stephens replied: "Then I am for war to the knife and the knife to the hilt." At all events, the commissioners returned here this morning and the peace mission is ended. We must now prepare to fight it out. And if all our people who are able to bear arms would go at once to the field, the war would be over in twelve months. You will doubtless see in the papers the true version of what occurred between Lincoln & Seward and our commissioners, before this reaches you. What I have heard is rumour. I will know, perhaps, tomorrow. I may add a few words to-morrow morning, and will write you again, perhaps, during the week. Good night dearest, good night.

Monday morning. I have your second letter of the 25th ult. I have also a letter from Mr. Clayton, informing me that he would send up immediately all my bonds & notes to you by express, and send also the interest which he has collected—(over nine hundred dollars). Pay Mattox for the pork purchased from him. Pay blacksmith's account. If you have it to spare send Col Martin five hundred dollars. I hope you have received the eight hundred dollars from Capt.

---

150. Brigadier General D. M. DuBose, formerly commanding officer of the 15th Ga. Regt. He was captured at Gettysburg, exchanged and in 1864 promoted to brigadier general. He succeeded to command of Wofford's brigade after the latter was assigned to the Department of Northern Georgia on January 20, 1865.

Scott. Out of it you may spare enough to do what I have said. You must keep enough for all current expenses. I obtained leave of absence to go home if I could not get my securities removed from Augusta, by a friend. This has been done and if I now leave it will be a violation of my promise. I *know you* would not have me do this. I am sorry I can not get home. I know you will be disappointed. I know I am, but I must do my *duty*, and, therefore, have to remain here awhile longer. I think I will have to stay at least until the first of March. I must stay until I vote on some important bills,—the tax bill, consolidation bill and a few others of great importance,—I feel it to be my *duty* to vote on these bills. Having leave of absence granted me I intend to leave here as soon as a sense of duty will allow it. If the road is cut so that I can not telegraph you when I am to leave here, I will go to Abbeville, and then to my cousin's and get him to send me home or over to Mr. Mattocks, and get him to send me home. So you need have no fears about my getting home. Columbia will have to be taken. If that was done, I could still go through to Abbeville or Anderson by wagon, or some other conveyance. The army officers are bound to furnish me transportation home when the usual mode and manner of travel is cut off. And if our forces fall back this side of Columbia, I can go to the army and demand transportation home, and the law requires transportation to be furnished me. You know not how anxious I am to go home. The President has just sent us the report of Stephens, Hunter & Campbell. Lincoln says we must *submit*. He refers to his message and proclamation. *Slavery must go*. That *he* will be *liberal* in granting *pardons* to the rebels. No commissioners were appointed by Lincoln. He and Seward met them on board a steamer in Hampton Roads. Lincoln says he will not treat with us, *nor with any separate State*. He says Congress of the U. S. has passed a law to amend the Constitution of the U. S. to abolish slavery,—*all slavery and all liberty* must be given up. But you will soon see the report in the papers. I have sent you a dispatch by telegraph to-day. Hope you will get it friday. I can fix no day when I will leave here. But you need not write to me but once after this is received. Write immediately, and then stop, for your letters will not reach me. Indeed I think you need not write at all, as it takes from eight to twenty days for a letter to reach me. And I think I will be at home in two weeks or less after you get this. I inclose a piece of paper, one half for Verdy and one half for Kate. Tell them I sent it to them. I write while the House is in session, and write at intervals. I will stop writing, and will write again to-morrow. Do not be uneasy about my getting sick. If I should get sick my colleagues will take care of me, and the ladies are polite and kind at my boarding house, and I think they would be attentive to me. But I'm not sick. My health is good, and I eat my rations with a zest. I am now anxious to dinner.

Good by dearest one. God bless you and all my children.

Your devoted husband
Warren Akin

Elberton Ga.
March 11th 1865

[To Nathan Land]

MY DEAR FRIEND: I reached home between seven and eight oclock P. M. on sunday last (the 5th inst) after a long and fatiguing journey through the country, most of the time in wagons. I travelled from Newton N. C. (look at your map) to Lincolnton, Shelby, Spartanburg & Greenville, in five different wagons – by rail road to Abbeville, and from Abbeville to this place in a wagon. The roads were the worst I ever travelled. It was all four horses could do to draw four men and their trunks, and we often walked to favor the horses. I walked as much as five or six miles in a day. The journey was a painful and an expensive one. We paid $150.*00* for two mules & wagons to go fifteen miles in. The rest of the wagons had four horses. My anxiety to reach home was very great. But my joy on arriving here was mingled with tears. My beloved Elbert was in his grave. O, my son, my son! How I desire to see him! About day break on the 2nd of Feby. I dreamed seeing him on the ground in blood. I know not how he came there. I ran to him and raised him up and a stream of blood ran out of his mouth. He seemed speechless, but not dead, and in much grief I exclaimed: "O, my boy, my boy!" I awoke much distressed, and continued depressed in feeling for some days. I wrote that day to my wife and told her my dream. When she received my letter my dream had been fulfilled, and my poor son was in his last resting place. Six days after I had the terrible dream, on the evening of the 8th of Feby. my son got on the poney of one of the school-boys to run him with another horse, and just before reaching the gate in front of my house, the saddle turned and he fell on the hard frozen ground. Mrs. Thomas being near him ran and raised him up and the blood poured out of his mouth, nose and ears. His right wrist was out of place, his right side injured, he was breathless and seemed to be dead. He however soon revived a little, but never spoke. This was wednesday. He lived until saturday morning (the 11th) half past ten oclock and breathed his last. Was buried the next day, Sunday, the 12th of Feby. He was unconscious from his fall and seemed to know no one or any thing. If I could have been with him, or he could have spoken and left some word for me, I could have borne it better. I can see him now as I saw him in my dream, and as he was in health. But how difficult it is for me to realize he is gone! What fond hopes were buried with him. My oldest son! Named in honor of my native county, sleeps beneath her sod. He had grown very fast recently, and was as tall as his mother. O, if he could have sent some word to me! I buried three children before, but I never wanted either of them back. But now I have prayed for dear Elbert's grave to open and for him to come forth. But, alas! he can not return to me, and my poor heart aches, aches. I miss him so much. He was my dependence – old enough to attend to nearly every thing for me. The last letter I received from him, written a short time before his death, was the longest and most intelligent one I ever received from him. It was a sort of diary, written on several different days. How sorry, sorry I am I did not preserve it. I heard nothing about his death or injury until I reached Abbeville. I received there a few lines saying he was dead, but giving no particulars. But I felt almost certain he was killed, and so stated to Col Bell[151] who was with me. How mysterious are the doings of Providence. Yet, I know, he "doeth all things well." I can not so see it, but I know it is so. O for patience and resignation to His will. The grief and anxiety of my poor wife have told heavily upon her, and she looks years older than she did three months ago. She and the baby have very bad colds, the rest well. My health as usual for me. Present me kindly to Mrs. Land and all the children,

Write to your much afflicted friend
Warren Akin

My wife received a few days since Mrs Land's letter written some weeks since and will answer it before long.

Elberton Ga.
May 15th 1865

Brig Genl Brown
Commanding U. S. Troops
at Hartwell Ga

GENERAL: I write to inquire whether you will parole me, or give me a writing that will protect me from arrest by U. States soldiers, and allow me to stay at home and attend to my own private affairs

151. Colonel Hiram P. Bell, 43rd Ga. Regt.

and professional business?[152] That you may act understandingly allow me to state to you who I am and my condition.

The people of the 10th Congressional District of this State elected me in 1863, to the Confederate States Congress. I attended the session in May 1864, and a part of the session last winter.

I was opposed to secession, and voted for and aided in electing delegates to the State convention, in Jany, 1861, who were opposed to it; but when Georgia seceded I felt it to be my duty to obey the command of my native State, and I did so faithfully and honestly. I could not stay in Georgia and be a secret traitor or an open enemy. While I thought I foresaw the dreadful consequences that would follow secession–without discussing the right of a sovereign State thus to act–I yet felt it to be my duty to go with Georgia and let her fate be mine. This opinion remains unchanged.

I have never been in the army or the militia service. I am too old and infirm for such duty.–being now in my fifty fourth year.

My health is far from being good. I have been in bad health for many years, and were I cast into prison I feel assured I could not live long.

I have a wife and six children, and as the U. S. soldiers have burnt up all my houses and office at Cassville, and taken from me considerable property, my family need my attention and assistance. Under these circumstances I request that you parole me and state in it that I may go any where in the State that my business calls me. I may desire to go into South Carolina.

General, I am not begging for mercy, but requesting, simply, the privilege you grant to the common soldier.

Mr. Akerman,[153] who will hand you this, is fully empowered to sign any paper that may be required in my behalf.

Trusting, sir, that this hastily written note will not be misunderstood,

I am, General, respectfully
Your obt. Sevt.
Warren Akin

152. The addressee, Brig. Gen. S. B. Brown, was in command of the occupation forces in the Elberton area. During the war he had commanded the 11th Michigan Cavalry.

153. Amos T. Akerman, a New Englander, educated at Dartmouth, came to Georgia to teach and stayed on to become a permanent resident of the state. Though opposed to secession, he served as a captain in the Confederate Army. He became a Republican after the war, and served for a short time in the Grant administration as Attorney General of the United States. At the time he wrote this letter he was a resident of Elberton.

May 17, 1865

Yesterday at Hartwell, I presented the above letter at the head quarters of Brevet Brig. Genl S. B. Brown commdy U. S. forces. The General not appearing, it was received and read by his adjutant, Capt. Van Bleak, who returned it to me, stating that a parole was unnecessary, and that if the statements in the letter were true, Mr. Akin, as long as he remained at home attending to his family and private business, would not be arrested or otherwise molested.

Amos T. Akerman

Brig Genl Brown

Courtesy of
Mr. Akerman

☆ 7 ☆

"My Dear Husband"

Elberton January 8th 1865

MY DEAR HUSBAND: I am not going to preaching today—if they have preaching, which is not certain, every time I get very cold my tooth ach begins, for that reason I will not go out to-day and then I want to write to you. Friday night I received six letters from you, five written during Christmas week and one of the 11th of December that last was the very one I've been wanting for a long time for you tell me in it how you live at your boarding house, how your room is furnished and various other little things that are not very important but are very interesting to me because it gives me a better idea of how you are living. In your letter of the 26th you tell me Mr. Clayton will send me some money by express I suppose I will get a letter from Mr. Clayton next mail day. The mail was so very late getting here Friday night I knew it would be useless to send to Major Jones to get him to see Mr. England for me and I had heard Mr. England did not bring the mail over, so I wrote a note to Mr. England and requested him to bring the money for me and asked him not to send by any one but a trusty person. I will write to Mr. Stokely about the money Capt. Dunlap Scott will send to me by the next mail. When the money comes I will let Mr. Mattox know I am ready to pay him, he will think the pork very cheap at $1.50 per lb. Major Jones says bacon will soon be selling at 8 or 10 dollars per lb and Mr. Gilreath says it will be 15 or 20 dollars per lb. I am glad you went to Anderson's bridgade and preached to the men. I want you to see Gen Lee so you can tell the children and me too how he looks. You must not forget to let me know what has become of Mr. Foot. I hope it may be true about Lee's being made commanding General of all our armies. the people have confidence in him, and so much has been said against Davis there is now a class of people who are ready at any moment to turn all they can against Davis and would be glad to see him killed, captured, or any other misfortune overtake him. I am shocked at the way the people here talk about him. They need Yankees here dreadfully, then they would cease their complaints against the President and those he puts in command of the armies and they would go to work to help defend the country. I am told that many of the militia near Augusta asked for permission to come home it was refused, and they came without. I know there are some here who done that, and others who are here and whose furlough has expired say they are not now going back. Every one I talk to is in favor of putting negros in the army and that *immediately*. Major Jones speaks very strongly in favor of it. I think slavery is now gone and what little there is left of it should be rendered as serviceable as possible and for that reason the negro men ought to be put to fighting and where some of them will be killed, if it is not done there will soon be more negroes than whites in the country and they will be the free race. I want to see them *got rid of soon.*

I am decidedly in favor of your some times going to an eating house and getting something to eat, from 9 'til five oclock is too long a time for you to stay without eating. I hope you will go every day when you get hungry and get some thing. Your pay has been increased a little and I believe you ought to spend it in whatever will contribute to your health & comfort. Your health ought to be your *first* care while in Richmond and if you fast so long you will eat too much when you get to your dinner & that may prove a serious disadvantage to you and might make you sick.

My dearest, you allude to the 12th of October /48, as being such a happy time. I feel with you in all you write, but the 25th of December 1860 was a happier day to me. Do you remember that on that day for the first time in two months you left your bed. I felt like you were as one restored to me from the dead almost, and when Rachel and I got you dressed and in your chair I began to feel an assurance that you would live many years to bless me and your children with your love and care and I assure you I was very happy.

I receive the Sentinel regularly now. I subscribed for the Tri-weekly Constitutionalist and for the Atlanta Registry.[154] I have received them for the last two mails. I am sorry to learn your socks are wearing out. Can you not get some woman to darn them for you. If your boots are worn so they are leaking, you ought to have them fixed never mind what it cost. It might save you a big doctor's bill. I wrote you in a former letter you had better not get that doll for Verdy. I still think it costs too much for you to get it but if you do get it just get the head and and I can make the rest, & it will not do to get Verdy a doll without getting one for Katie too. Perhaps you might for 10 or 20 cents in silver get a small head, that used to be the price of them.

You write of the number of women who are to be seen on the streets at night. I am not surprised at that. They have nothing to fear

---

154. Mrs. Akin was doubtless referring to the Atlanta *Register* (1862-1865).

from those who make it a business to rob men. I am glad to know you dont go out at night. I am always fearing some accident might happen to you if you go out at night. You ask how many letters I have received from you. I have now before me sixteen and I think I have kept them all. Like you I almost wish some one of us would get sick enough to bring you home but still I take good care of myself and the children and hope our Doctor's bill for this year will be a very small one. Doctor Jones came to see Joe Shackleford's baby once while she was here and charged her $5.00 for the visit. He and Shackleford are second cousins. You mention going to see Dr. Dogget. I did not know till you mentioned going to see him that he had called on you. I am truly glad to know you have some pleasant acquaintances, hope you may visit frequently. It will make the time pass off more quickly and pleasantly and then you will have more to tell me when you come home.

I've tried to answer two of your letters I have the one of the 28th & 29th before me and will try to answer that. Your suggestions about my writing to you are very good but I have so many things to attend to, such a cross baby and Lotty is such a poor nurse if I were to write as often as you tell me to I would have no time to sew, knit, or mend clothes, and then as you truly say "there are some things I would like to tell you but fear to write them." I am rather inclined to think if the LC [?] rail road by Augusta is not threatened by the enemy and Augusta is not in immediate danger you had better come by Lexington and not by Abbeville. If the Savannah river was up very high would it be safe for you to cross there, that is my objection to your coming by Abbeville, the roads are very bad any way you may come.

The mules are in tolerably good order I've had their manes & tails trimmed nicely and if talking will make Bob curry them they will be well curried. They are well fed. I think they have too much corn, but Bob and the boys think differently. Must I give thirty dollars a load for shucks? If I got the boys up in time to take the keys out to Bob I would have to go to their beds and give them a whipping every morning. I have enough corn got out every night to feed in the morning. I take the stable key off the bunch and let Bob get that very early to feed the mules. In spite of all I can say he will send Allen for the key and some times I have detected Allen in taking all the keys from the nail where they hung. I now put all but the stable key under my pillow. Warren attends to feeding cow. She is in good order is well fed but does not give over three quarts of milk. She is a vicious bad cow and keeps me out of the horse lot often when I want to go there. Two weeks ago I had three hens laying. I can not get the eggs of but one now. I have bought a few chickens since you left, can not get hens, or Bob says he can find none to buy. I have the hen house cleaned out frequently, have had nests [?] fixed on the ground. The pigs look very well indeed, they get plenty to keep them very fat without boiling their food for them. I think they are of a very small breed of hogs. We rarely here rats now they are still very bad in the pantry and smoke house. The cat Bob brought here will soon have an increase in her family and I want to get rid of her now. If I do not we will have too many cats and they will eat chickens when we have them. Warren's kitten has run away or been stolen. Some one threw John's in the fire and burnt its feet badly. Katie's "Thomas" has commenced to fatten and improve Katie is as proud of him as ever. I will remember your instructions about the garden when I commence work there. Bob shows a disposition to be as mean as possible about any work I may want him to do. I will do the best I can tho' about all the work at home. I am very glad you wrote so much about what ought to be done in the garden and the lots. I wish as you think of such things you would say all you can to remind me of what ought to be done. I have not been near as smart as I intended when you left home. I have tooth ache & ear ache so often I shrink from the cold and often I expect excuse myself from any domestic duties on that score when I ought [not] to do so. The cross fence has been fixed up long since Bob has not quite finished the horse lot fence. Elbert wants you to know he & Warren helped Floyd cut all the posts, and they have cut wood too.

I am truly glad to know you have such good health and feel strong & *young*. I have excellent health but I dont feel young at all, and I am sure I look old, my hair will soon be white. It is very gray now and gets more so every week I think. I have tried to answer your letters as they were written. I've answered four of them and now have yours of the 29th before me to answer. I do not think I will get cousin Sally's barouch too often. I was sorry I had to get it to send Joe Shackleford to Ruckersville, but I was obliged to. Joe's baby was too unwell & the weather too bad for her to go in the wagon, and I wanted her to leave, her visit was very pleasant but being in the Christ- . . . [part of letter missing] twelve and one oclock and then I have supper about six oclock or a little after, the children generally sit up till 9 oclock. You see that getting up as early as we do and so many little children that want to eat often, it would be a waste of flour bread, and other things too to have two meals a day. the children would all want to eat before breakfast, before dinner, and after supper too. Mrs. Haire told me they had tried it and found it was not a good plan. Now a family of grown folks it would be just what we ought to have but it is no saving where there are so many little ones. Lucy cooks dinner and supper, Charlotte cooks breakfast then goes right to spinning spins 'till 8 oclock at night and never spins more than two and half cuts a day.

Mrs. Haire told me her Mother heard that Mrs. Chunn[155] had been back to Cassville and she supposed found she could not live there for she (Mrs. Chunn) returned to Grantville where she is keeping house now. Elliott could tell me none of the particulars of Mrs. Chunn's visit.

I received a letter for you from Mr. Seals[156] last Friday. he writes in answer to a letter you wrote him a long time ago, says his little son's illness then his own prevented his answering your letter sooner, he has had a long attack of typhoid fever, he says he can not pay the note you wrote about, and does not know when he can pay it as he has not made any more money than was necessary to pay his own family expenses and does not intend to try to make any by speculation. He says he intends trying to get back to Bartow in the Spring. he wrote a very friendly letter.

Monday night - I am sure my dear, you will not complain that this is a short letter I think it is a very long one for me to write. Today I wrote a note to Mr. Overton Tate making some inquiry about letting us have some land to cultivate and I also asked him to send the remainder of the pork you engaged of him as soon as the weather was suitable for saving it he was not at home his wife sent me word he would return in a few days and would then let me know what he could do about the land. I sent to Mr. Walls to-day for a load of corn the roads are so very bad Bob can not bring over 18 or 20 bushels at a load. he still has five or six loads to bring. I know it ought to have been brought home long ago, but Bob was determined not to hurry himself before Christmas and since that time the weather has been too bad to do any hauling. I hope Mr. Gilreath will hire Charles out soon he is so lazy and disobedient I can do nothing with him. I dont believe I ever saw as lazy a negro as he is. If Gilreath can not hire him out what must I do with him? I have written you how uneasy I feel about your being in Richmond now. I some times feel dreadfully distressed about it and unnecessarily unhappy. I so much fear the city will be taken or given up while you are there. I see in one

155. Mrs. Chunn was probably the widow of Samuel Love Chunn (died on Sept. 8, 1863). For a sketch of Chunn, see Cunyus, *History of Bartow County*, 52.

156. Probably Thomas A. Seals, listed in the 1860 census as a Cassville teacher, or Richard D. Seals, a Cass County farmer.

of the Sentinels that a resolution was introduced to adjourn on the 24th of this month what has been done about it? Oh my dear how I do wish you could be at home now. I am sitting by your little table writing, all are in bed and asleep but me. I can not sleep well while you are away and often have distressing dreams about you. You can never know all the anxious thoughts I have about you when you are away from home. You must continue to write often and write me long letters. they are my principal source of pleasure in your absence. I will stop for to night and finish my letter tomorrow. Good night dear husband.

Tuesday evening it is now quite late and I will not wait till the mail is opened to finish my letter but will send it to the office and answer your letter I may get this evening tomorrow and send it by Washington. Little Susie is growing finely she is a very smart sweet little thing Warren & Mary often quarrel about which shall hold her. they are more fond of her than the other children are. Last night we had one of the hardest rains here that I have ever known to fall. I fear it has damaged your wheat considerably, the wheat does not look well. I fear it will be but a poor lot.

We are all well. Your own devoted wife

Mary F. Akin

Elberton, January 15th 1865

MY DEAR HUSBAND: Last Friday night I received letters from Mrs. Land and brother Will, and four from you. Yours were dated the 21st December the 2nd 3rd & 5th of January. I have them all before me now to try to answer them and to tell you what Mrs. Land & brother Will said in their letters. Mrs. Lands letter looked like it had been through a good deal before it got here. She wrote as if she had heard direct from Mrs. Chun since her return from Cassville. She says their house is certainly burned and Tom Word is living in the kitchen their piano & carpet are at Dr. Harely's house and other things they left scattered about in different places None of the out houses at the Land's or Mrs. Chun's place were burnt. Mrs. Chunn says (The great cry of the people there is for bread they do not expect meat are perfectly satisfied if they can get bread.) Mrs. Land and her children are more anxious than ever to get back to Bartow County. Mr. Land has sold Oscar his wife & children, four of them, for twenty thousand dollars. The Lands live in a little log cabin with five rooms in it & one fire place Lila & her children are with them, and Mrs. L says they have "pushing times this cold weather." her letter was dated the 1st Jan. She mentioned that William Chunn had written to them since the battle of Franklin. he went over the field after the battle was over and said it was a dreadful sight. that is all she said about him. Old Mr. Best had started back to Bartow to look after what he left there.

Brother W.[157] is low spirited and finds it hard to live. he says "I am perfectly horrified at the idea of putting our negros in the army to fight. they will turn against us as soon as they can." and I think there is much truth in that but we are like the man with the elephant, and I am wanting to see them put where they will stand some chance of being killed as well as white folks. brother W. adds "None but those whose fears dictate this policy can think of such a course." he also says with truth "we could not be whipped if the people would do their duty. I am alarmed but it is the conduct of the people and our own public men that has done it." he says Pleas was at Freeman's during Shermans march through Ga. left there for Savannah and must have got there about the time the city fell since then has not been heard from. I hope he is safe but can not help having some fears about him. I never hear from Pa's family now. I have written frequently but get no answer to my letters. I have written you that Mr. Gilreath hired Floyd for 300 lbs of pork. Today I received a note from the man he is hired to about his clothes and shoes. Mr. Gilreath has given him no winter shoes and he needs some very much. I wrote to Mr. Campbell (that is the way he signs his name tho' he is called Kimbal) that if he would get a pair of shoes for Floyd I would pay him for them. I asked Gilreath about the clothes and he said he would make it all straight with you, and I have no doubt he will be willing to pay me what I have to pay Kimbal for the shoes. Yesterday Mr. Gilreath hired Charles for 200 lbs of pork to a Mr. William Bullard. Mr. Bullard is to clothe & shoe him and pay doctor's bill. Now Floyd & Charles are both hired out do you still wish to get land from Mr. Tate for Bob to cultivate. if Bob does cultivate any he will have to be much smarter than he has been any time lately. he seems to think hauling wood is all he has to do this year. I thought I mentioned that brother W. sent Emily home on a visit. I had rather he had not done so but its past now and makes no difference. I do not want Emily at home and wish I could hire out Allen & Rachel too.

I have not yet received the money from Capt. Scott or from Mr. Clayton, & Mr. England says there was nothing of the kind for me last Friday morning at the Lexington Depot. I suppose I will get both packages this week. I am glad you went to the President's levee. Last

---

157. Mrs. Akin's brother, William M. Verdery.

night I dreamed of going to a levee of President Davis' to look for you. I saw many persons I knew but could not find the one I was looking for & was having much trouble about it when Rachel came and woke me to tell me it was time to get up. In your letter of the 3rd you say you could write me news but fear to risk it in a letter. I expect you are right but I am sorry it is so you can not write whatever you feel like telling me. I have not been to see Mrs. Martin have not yet had the mule worked to the buggy and I know Mrs. M would not thank me for coming in a wagon to see her. By the way dont you think your friends here have rather slighted me this past Christmas. they had dining & teas among the married folks and never once gave me an invitation to any of their social gatherings. Now I dont care and would not have gone if they had invited me, but I think it would have been no more than common courtesy demanded of them, especially as they seem to think so much of you, and I doubt not if you had been at home you would have been invited all about and perhaps I would too. But these folks here dont know what real true politeness is.[158]

I am glad you got a letter from Col. Prather and I do hope he will be promoted. may be some of these days if he is made a Brigadier he may give one of our boys a position on his staff. What do you expect to do with Elbert when he is sixteen. I know you had rather I would say nothing about him to you but I feel so anxious about him I can not always keep silent. I have heard that old Mr. Lofton will open his school for boys very soon. I have also heard he is going to charge enormously high for tuition. I wish I knew whether I ought to go to see him about Elbert & Warren's schooling or write to him or what I ought to do. Ellize will start to Mr. Harris tomorrow. *Must she take music lessons.*

I am much gratified to know you have seen Gen Lee and been introduced to him. The children too are glad you have seen him. Mr. Gilreath told me old Mr. Glenn had written a letter to the Conference encouraging them to send preachers to northwestern Ga. he said he had by the Yankees & our own soldiers lost everything he had and was living on bread & water, but he begged conference to send a preacher to them, one who was willing to suffer with them & preach for them and he would be satisfied. Mr. Arbogast is Presiding elder in the same district old Mr. Glenn was. I have not yet learned the

---

158. Refugees in all parts of the Confederacy commonly complained of unfriendliness on the part of permanent residents. The coming of the refugees sometimes caused inconveniences for local folk and the increased demand for scarce necessities tended to push up prices.

name of the preacher who was sent on the Cassville circuit. Mr. Austin goes to Washington Wilkes and Mr. Grogan takes his place here.[159] Mr. Grogan has recently had considerable property left him in this county by old man Harris' son. I understand that is why he was sent here. When I see Mr. Austin he can tell me more about the preachers. Mrs. Austin told me to-day she & Mr. Austin were comnig to see me before they left here. I went to church today and heard Mr. Grogan preach a good plain sermon.

Johnny has fallen down and hurt his nose badly. he now picks up books and papers and tries to read. he says over the letters and when he comes to a comma he says "dot with a tail" when he comes to a semi colon or colon he says "two dots" when he comes to a period he say "dot." He is a very hard child to manage and I think the constant teasing he has to take from his brothers, particularly from Warren, makes him so, and I think it has very seriously affected his health. He looks very badly is thin and sallow and often complains of feeling sick. I have talked to both these boys about it and have almost frightened them about John's health and they are not so bad as they have been to tease and frighten him. It is now getting late Cousin Sally and Cora came up after supper and sat awhile with us. I was very glad to see her, it made me feel like I was at home to have a friend to come in as she did to night. We talked a good deal but said nothing I can remember to write for we talked on indifferent subjects. She never abuses the President to me. I like her very much altho' she does abuse the President and thinks children nuisances.

When I last wrote you I was almost sick. I feel quite well again. Susie has been sick. I gave her calomel and she now seems as well as usual. She laughs aloud & notices a great deal. I do wish you could see the dear little thing. Katie sleeps with me every night and is a troublesome baby. What will we do with her when you come.

Monday Eliza started to school this morning. she tells me Mr. Harris charges provisions for his tuition or its equivalent in money and she did not ask him how much provisions of any kind he would charge. If Mr. Lofton charges in that way too the tuition for the three children will be enormous.

---

159. The Reverend James M. Austin, Methodist minister of the Georgia Conference, served Elberton and the Colored Mission there in 1863-1864. In 1865 he was transferred to the Wilkes Circuit and Colored Mission. The Reverend John H. Grogan succeeded Austin as minister of the Elberton Methodist Church and Colored Mission. Information obtained by Willard E. Wight from Minutes of Georgia Conferences, 1864-1865.

Mr. Gilreath told me Wright Carswell[160] had been made Col of a Reg in uper Ga and he flourishes around Athens drinking & frolicing extensively. Now if such as he can so easily be made Col. what ought such men as Jack Prather to be? Jack had better go home and raise a Reg for local defence too. Mr. Gilreath told me Mrs. Latimer was still at Mr. Haire's. They all want to get away from there but I dont know where they will go to. Elliott said they would like very much to go to Madison.

Mary Verdy says "It takes father a long time to come home. I am afraid he is in a prisoner" she means in prison. John says he "thinks you have been a Congress man long enough." I have written a long letter. hope I will hear from you again this evening. I will certainly write again to-morrow. As ever my dearest.

Your devoted wife
Mary F. A

Elberton January 19th 1865

MY DEAR HUSBAND: Yesterday I received no letter from you I suppose it was because the railroads were so much damaged by the heavy rain we had about ten days since that no Richmond mails have come through to Ga. I did not receive any Richmond papers either. I hope you have received my letters I have written you two real long letters. When I dont get letters from you I do not know how to write much. I dont think I ought to tell you all the little things that happen at home that would annoy you and would do no good for me to be telling. I had rather not write anything that would be the least disagreeable to you. But I must mention some things that are mutually interesting to us and that are disagreeable too. Today I was looking at the wheat and it looks so badly, particularly the white wheat. I am fearful it will all have to be plowed up and planted in corn. The heavy rains washed the field very badly and then the hard freezes we have had has injured all wheat. What we have for this years use goes very fast and I have been eating more corn bread than anything else since Christmas, and we use a great deal of that, so much I felt fearful you had not engaged enough corn and tried to get Mr. Wall to let us have 15 or 20 bushels more, but he said he could not let me have any more. he told Bob he intended next week to ask $20.00 a bushel for corn. I am told it was last week selling for $12.00 per

160. No "Wright" Carswell could be positively identified. Reuben W. Carswell, formerly a lieutenant colonel of the 48th Ga. Regt., in 1864 was brigadier general of Georgia State Troops. See L. L. Knight, *A Standard History of Georgia and Georgians* (Chicago, 1917), IV, 2073.

bushel. The other day I was at Mrs. Swift's, her brother in law Mr. Harper came in. I had heard that he had shucks to sell. I asked him what he would let me have a load for and he said $50.00. Ought I to give that for shucks?

I have returned the calls of all these ladies in town. I went a few evenings since to see old Mrs. Henry. her son Capt Henry was also at Mr. Vail's and I heard him say that it was the general belief in the Army that Richmond would be evacuated the army withdrawn from Virginia and brought to the cotton States. Capt Henry seems to be an intelligent man. I ought to have mentioned that old Mrs. Henry is Mrs. Vails mother and she lives with Mrs. Vail. the same evening I was there quite a little crowd of ladies came in and they all seem to enjoy talking of themselves and their own affairs very much. most of the conversation was unintelligible to me for they talked of people I did not know and called most of them by their given names, and therefore I did not stay very long. This evening I went to see Cousin Sally but as usual she had gone visiting. she loves to visit, and I believe most of the ladies here visit a good deal. When I found Cousin Sally was not at home I went on to see old Mrs. Thomas. she took too much morphine the other day or it was stronger than usual and it made her quite sick for a few days. she looks badly and had just left her bed when I called in to see her. She seemed very glad to see me. the lady who lives with and takes care of her, Mrs. Horton, is a very pleasant woman. I have worked some on my scrap book but not so much as I want to, indeed I have so much sewing to do and so many babies to wait on and watch and work for, and so many little housekeeping affairs to attend to, I dont have much time for my scrap book or for reading, and not as much time as I wish for writing, right now I ought to quit writing and reel the broaches Charlotte has just brought in. Yesterday I had a few Irish potatos planted and I have sowed cabbage seed. today I had manure scattered over the squares in the garden and had it plowed up. I am exceedingly anxious to have an early and good garden and expect to work well at it when ever the weather will permit. I think it best not to work the stawberry bed but just have the little peach & plum trees dug up and after awhile have the square cleaned off. Tomorrow I have to send Bob to mill with wheat & corn and the next day I am going to have the grape vines and currant bushes trimmed. I dont know anything about currants and am rather inclined to think they ought not to be trimmed much. I will also have the raspberry vines trimmed.

Thursday morning) Bob and Elbert have just started to the mill and

John went with his brother. Elbert has got uneasy about Johnny and lately has taken great care of him, makes him cut wood with him, play marbles and run about with him, and I think it does Johnny much good. Tuesday night I received a letter from Capt Scott telling me he had sent that eight hundred dollars to me at Lexington Depot. I immediately wrote to Mr. Little and requested him to send it to me by Mr. England or any other person who might be passing and who was reliable. I sent the note to him by Mr. England as it was too late for me to mail it. I suppose I will get the money tomorrow. Dont you think it rather strange I get no letters from Ala neither does brother Will. I want to go to see brother Will soon after you come home. I was more anxious than you can ever know to go last year, but you objected until it was too late for me to go. I hope you will not only be willing but will help me to get there this year. It has been a long time since I have been to see any of my relatives and it is a great relief to some times get away from home.

I have enquired among all the ladies I have seen about the boys school they all say they have heard it is to commence before long, but no one seems to know anything certain about it. I suppose some one will teach and when they begin I will hear of it and will start the boys to school immediately. I wish they could be going now. the people here seem very indifferent about schooling their children. Elbert received a letter from Carolin Heath last Friday he would let none of us see it and said there was no news in it. So I supposed Carolin wrote about Sally. Elbert answered the letter right off.

Thursday night.) This morning I called on Mrs. Marcus Bell found her a very pleasant and talkative refugee, says she never saw people need to suffer from Yankees as these do, she says no one seems willing to sell them anything unless they get a fortune for it. I went to Mr. Vail's store to buy a few needles, and I bought some jeans there at $18.00 per yd, he had some very inferior at $12.00 pr yd, and a very good piece for $20.00 per yd. I think I ought to get that last mentioned piece too, but I did not need it immediately and did not have money enough to pay for it and then I did not know what you would say to it. But if I had *plenty* of money & felt like I could do as I pleased with it I would get that jeans for if I did not want to use it I could soon sell it for 25 or 30 dollars a yd. Mr. Chapman was here yesterday came to see when you were coming home. While here he told me he had recently been to Athens and had bought some factory thread and I engaged two bunches of it from him for $56.00 a bunch. It is selling here at $100.00 per bunch or 25 lbs of bacon if its paid in that. Spools of thread sell here for $10.00 per spool, needles from 10 to 20 dollars a paper. I tell you when I have a needle taken from my cushion now I am angry and scold shamefully. This evening I went to see Mrs. Bruce a little while she has a sick child. While in the Vail's store this morning Mr Hester came up and spoke to me he asked particularly about you, asked if I was not uneasy about your safety, and also told me the Yankees had taken Pocataligo and it was thought they would advance on Augusta. Dearest I can not help feeling much anxiety about you, and I do so long for the time to come for you to get home. When do you think you can leave Richmond. I hope it will not be long before I get a letter from you saying you are coming home. Sometimes, especially at night after the children are gone to bed, I get so uneasy about you I can not help feeling very unhappy, but I try to feel reconciled to your absence and if I just could know when you were coming home I could bear your absence better. I will stop writing for tonight and hope I will get letters from you tomorrow.

Always dearest, Your devoted wife,
Mary F. Akin

P. S.

Mr. Bruce sent me word this morning that the Yankees had taken Fort Fisher. If that is so I suppose Wilmington will fall then will not Richmond be evacuated. dont stay in Richmond too long my dear. I dreamed last night you had come home this evening and we were all very happy together. I hope that dreamed may very soon be realized

☆ 8 ☆

"The Children Make a Dreadful Fuss Around Me"

Elberton January 22nd 1865

MY DEAR HUSBAND, Another mail day has passed and I have received no letter from you. I see by the Augusta papers that nearly all the railroads between here and Richmond are very much damaged by the heavy rain we had two weeks ago and some fears are expressed about getting supplies for the army to Virginia. Sherman is advancing on Branchville and will no doubt take that place. Fort Fisher has fallen and all these things make me fear you may be cut off from home and then I know not what I should do, as it is I fear I will not be able to hear from you in a long time. If Branchville is taken by the enemy how will the mail from Virginia reach Augusta?

Friday night I received a letter from Ma. her letter was commenced on the 19th December and finished on the 4th of this month. The company of old men that Pa belongs to had been tendered to Gov Watts to go where ever he chose to send them. When the raid was made on Pollard they were [order]ed [MS torn] there to meet the Yankees. they went and were in two battles with the Yankees before reinforcements arrived. at first they were repulsed and had to retreat, but the second time held the Yankees in check until reinforcements arrived and assisted in driving them off. there were about 200 of our men and from 600 to 2,000 Yankees. I am very sorry Pa ever joined a company. it was altogether unnecessary and he is so much needed at home he ought to stay there, and he is now 62 years old. Virginia is very unhappy because she left her home and came to Pa's, talks about going back. she was badly treated by Troup and old man Witcher too, and Abner Darden never noticed a letter she wrote him and she could not see him. she had to manage for herself the best she could in selling what she did and in getting away from Cedar Valley. Sister is still teaching at Major Good's. Ory has not yet gone to teaching. Addy has gone back to her school near Montgomery. George can now walk with a stick he has not yet received his pay, gets nothing but his rations, why is that. Are none of the retired officers paid? Of course Pa has to help George live now and

I dont see how he can support all that are with him now and hes hiring negroes to help him too. I believe I have written all that Ma wrote that would interest you She had not heard when she wrote that Pleasant had gone to Savannah about the time the city fell, thought he was still with Free. I feel quite anxious about Pleas, but hope he is safe.

Eliza and Elbert went to church today. I did not go, the weather is very bad and I fear tooth ache so much I dont go out anywhere when the weather is so bad. Mr. Tate has not yet sent the meat. I do not know why for we have had beautiful weather for saving pork & he told me he would send it this past week. I hope it will come soon.

Elbert wants you to bring him a box of caps and he says he dont care if you bring him and his brother some powder. I have made a coat for Elbert out of the jeans left of making your coat. it was a very scant patern but after [?] cutting and peicing a good deal I got a coat. I have not yet received the money you sent me by Capt Scott or that you ordered to be sent me from Augusta. I have written a note to Mr. Little sent it by mail and I hope to get the money next Tuesday. I have written to Mrs. Land and to Virginia. It has been some three weeks since I wrote to Mrs. Best and a month since I wrote to Mrs. Shepherd. I have not yet received answers to my letters. You have never told who the letters were from that you received by flag of truce, tell me in your next letter who they were from. and tell me if any thing has been done for Feaster Woolley or Emory Best.

Last Friday Eliza received a letter from John Land asking her to correspond with him, just to think of that. Eliza asked me what she should do, and as it was John, I told her to write to him if she chose to do so that it was a correspondence she could drop whenever she thought proper, and she has written to him. Did you think John could be induced to write to a young lady. Elbert and Warren have laughed most heartily about John's writing to their Sister and I expect you will laugh too. Eliza also received a letter from George Latimer. he was at Pocataligo when he wrote.

Monday night) Hearing yesterday that old Mr. Lofton would open his school this morning I started the boys to school today. Mr. Macarty was there to let the boys know the school could not begin to day because old Mr. Lofton had just heard that his son, Col John Lofton, was killed at Fort Fisher.[161] I suppose the school will be

161. Col. John T. Lofton, 6th Ga. Regt. Fort Fisher, near Wilmington, N. C., was attacked by the Federals in mid-January, 1865, and was captured on February 15.

opened tomorrow and I will start the boys again. they are very unwilling to go to school, but it is so important for them to learn now I will send them whenever I can. My dear, you can not know how exceedingly anxious I am for you to get home. I think your presence is much needed and then I do have such a very lonely time while you are away and I am living among strangers. I know you are homesick and almost crazy sometimes to get home, but then you are kept so busy you do not often have a chance to sit down & think of home, and you know too we are all in a place of comparative safety, but while I sit and sew or nurse children I think of you all the time and knowing that the enemy are so [determined to ?] [MS torn] take Richmond I fear for your safety all the time. You can never know how many sad and anxious hours I spend thinking of you, and it has now been a long time since I heard from you. Your last letter was dated the 5th of January and I do not know when I will get a letter from you again. I hope I will get a good many from you to morrow and if I do not I am sure I will be sick with anxiety about you, or I ought to say I fear it will make me sick. Verdy has a cold and cough but is not sick. I believe Katie is worse to cry for me to hold and nurse her now she has ever been. She sleeps with me, and dont want me to nurse Susie at all while she is awake. Eliza has slept in my room ever since you went away and Mary sleeps with her. I have a fire in the dining room at night & in the morning. I try to be as economical with the wood as possible, but it goes very fast, and I am some times inclined to think it is not all burnt here. Mrs. Dobbs send me the Atlanta Intelligencer[162] frequently and then gets our papers to read she is still up and going about. I thought she would have been confined long since. I have not seen David Dobbs Jr in a long time. he is here, but I have not seen him when I went to see his wife. Some time ago when I wrote to you I told you if you felt able to afford it I wished you to get a calico dress for me and for Eliza. did you ever get them? I do not wish you to get the dress for me unless my dear, you think you can afford it.

Did you ever get that doll for Verdy. I wrote you I thought perhaps you had better not get it and think she will not expect it when I tell her you can get none to suit her. She grows very fast and is now large for her age. She says "I wonder what's the reason it takes father so long to come home." Johnny answers her "Why he aint done Congress yet." Then she always expresses great fear that the

162. Atlanta *Intelligencer* (1854-1891). The *Intelligencer* was published in Macon for a few months following the fall of Atlanta, but resumed publication in Atlanta early in December, 1864. See Garrett, *Atlanta and Its Environs*, I, 665, 661.

Yankees will get you. I put an apple away for you to give Katie when you come, but I fear it will not keep much longer. She always says "Fawer's doing to bring me a big nice apple" Last week I bought three hens and a rooster, two of the hens are laying. I gave sixteen dollars for the four. I have two hens setting one under the house the other under the . . . [MS torn]
night sometimes he leaves before my supper's over and I dont [see him when] he comes back. I have never said a word to him about it, but I . . . [MS mutilated] he is so consistently away at night. Ought I to say anything to him about it [dearest] [?] I will now quit writing for to night if I think of any thing more I ought to write I will write it to morrow.

Your ever devoted wife,
Mary F. Akin

Tuesday

I started the boys to school again this morning Old Mr. Lofton told them he felt so distressed about his son's death he could not teach this week but would begin next Monday morning. Bob is hauling some peas to-day for Mr. Bruce [?], the ground is too wet for him to plow or work in the garden and I let him haul for Bruce. Mr. Wall has promised me another load of shucks and I expect to send for them tomorrow Mrs. Brannon [?] proposes to let me keep the table that is here if I will pay for having a smaller one made for her, and I will do as she proposes about it. I will write again very soon. Your loving wife,

MFA.

Elberton January 25 1865

MY DEAREST HUSBAND: Today I wrote you a short letter and sent it by Washington I did not have time to take your letters and try to answer them and was feeling very badly too. I sent you Mr. Tate's note declining to take the interest bearing treasury notes as he did not know what they were worth. I got but a half load of shucks from Mr. Wall to-day but the promise of two more loads after awhile. He also declines taking interest bearing treasury notes says he has more on hand of that kind of money than he has any use for, says he "will take new issue when persons are anxious to pay. but he prefers a good note of hand of anything else." I doubt not Mattox's answer will be the same as the others.

In your letter of the 6th you say you "would willingly walk ten miles [through] dark & mud to see me" I dont think you could very well walk that far any time unless you have improved in strength very much. Did you answer the letters you received by flag of truce and what did you say to the man who wished flour sugar bacon & tobacco. You say I've never mentioned but one letter as having been received for you. I certainly mentioned that one came from Cobb directly after you went away in which he said he would bring that money to me if he did not see you before you left. But he has never brought the money and I dont suppose he will bring it now, and I also told you of my having received a letter for you from Mr. Seals, and that is all that have come for you since you went away. I am surprised you do not get my letters I have lately written you some very long ones I think I wrote you one of eight pages and on paper like this too. I know that satisfied you in quantity and perhaps quality too. I am truly sorry for Mark Hardin and his poor wife, there have been many exchanges of prisoners since he was captured and it seems to me he ought to have been among those exchanged. I am fearful there is more favor than justice shown in that as well as in many other things. If more justice had been practiced in our army and Government we would now have been more successful

My dear, all you express to me in your letter of the 8th I have felt about the condition of the country. It has been a long time since I saw any prospect of a happy termination of the war for us, and I look for subjugation *for a while* and all its attendant horrors as our fate. Do you not remember that more than two years ago almost three, you spoke of selling what little specie you had then and I objected because I feared then it would some day be all we had of worldly possessions, and even that our cruel enemies may make useless to us. I have thought of these things for so long a time and so much too, I have partially prepared myself for the worst, but there is one thing I can not think of with any calmness or fortitude and that is the cruel fate that may be in store for you if we should fail in this dreadful struggle for national existence. I am truly glad that you have written so freely of what you think and fear, it gives me much food for thought and I hope you will continue to do so. In the letter I wrote this morning I told you how violently Elbert was opposed to entering the Naval School. Old Mr. Lofton told him & Warren to study this week at home and they have been at their books all day to day. In your letter of the 10th you regret that I write in such a complaining tone. You are mistaken, when I simply tell you what is not agreeable I dont think that is complaining. You also say you regret I allowed Rachel to have a dance at her house. I think you would have done just as I did if you had been at home. It is hard to refuse such a servant as Rachel anything, and you know how very kind and attentive she has been to me during all the trouble sickness and fatigue I had moving here and during my confinement too. and then my dear I never hear you refuse your servants anything they ask of you, and I think you do right about it and I try in all things to do as you would if you were home. I felt sure I told you in some of my letters that Joe Shacklefords baby was a big boy, twice as large as Susie. Mr. Shackleford is with the malitia and has not been home yet unless it is very lately. Joe had not seen him when she was here since last September. I thought you knew long ago that Joe Hardin was separated from her husband. I am told she "flies around" as gay as a young widow, goes to Milledgeville and every where else she can and has a string of beau following her every where. Joe Shackleford told me that last piece of news about her. Joe had not named her baby when she was here and he is as ugly as babies can get to be. I have noticed no call in the papers for a meeting of the Legislature next month but perhaps when they adjourned in such haste they resolved then to meet in Feb. I see by the papers that Jesse Glenn on his responsibility broke up the meeting that was to call for a convention in Jackson County. If those men in Thomas County who held that meeting could have a Yankee army to pass thro' that section of country they would soon have all such feelings as wishing to treat with such an enemy knocked out of them. Last night Mr. Bruce and his wife came down to see me and sat an hour we had a pleasant time. Mr. Bruce tells me he heard from Mr Marcus who has just got home from Augusta that all the Government stores are being moved from that city. I suppose you have seen Gen Hardee's order about the cotton in Augusta,[163] it is a great pity he did not give similar orders about the cotton in Savannah and had it burnt too . . . [MS torn-] said that Sherman has already got tired of the kindness

163. No order of Hardee's for the destruction of cotton in Augusta was found, though it was the policy of the Confederate Government to burn cotton thought likely to fall into Federal possession. On Jan. 21, 1865, Secretary of War James A. Seddon ordered D. H. Hill, in command at Augusta, to do all that he could to induce the removal of cotton from that city. Seddon stated: "To promote removal and to be prepared for contingencies, make preparations to burn whatever cotton may be in the city in the event of its evacuation or capture. It must not fall into the hands of the enemy." Henceforth there was much excitement and discussion in Augusta about the prospect of the cotton being destroyed. See Florence Fleming Corley, "Augusta, Georgia, A Confederate City" 175; also *Official Records*, ser. 1, XLVII, pt. 2, 1032, and ser. 4, III, 1066-1067.

Failure to destroy the cotton at Savannah before that city fell to the Federals led the Confederate War Department, on request of the Confederate House of Representatives, to ask General Hardee for an explanation. On February 6, 1865, Hardee informed the Richmond authorities that, owing to the manner in which the cotton was stored in Savannah, it could not have been burned without destroying the city. See *Official Records*, ser. 1, XLVII, pt. 2, 1105 and LIII, 412.

with which he preferred to treat the people in Savannah and now the negroes and Yankees are robbing the citizens of everything and treating them shamefully. If it is true I do not know that I am sorry they will not now be so anxious to get back in the Union. I am disheartened when I read of so much fault finding and complaint against the Government as there is all over the state that is what defeats our army. So much fault finding is obliged to have a demoralizing effect on the soldiers in the field.

Thursday) Yesterday Mr. Tate sent me three hogs. I had them cut up and salted down last night. I am having the lard dried up and other things attended to to day and the weather is very very cold. we have had none colder this winter. I have Bob hauling up some wood this morning and Cousin Sally has asked for him and the mules this evening. she wishes to have the mules hitched to her carriage and go out in the county this evening. She dont mind the weather at all. And I have promised to let Mr. Perry Bruce have the wagon to take him over to Lexington Friday he is to pay me $50.00 for the trip and the next time I expect to charge $75.00 it is worth it. I have had a little hauling done for Mr. Sidney Bruce, he says he will pay anything I charge I have got him to do some work on the harness and when he wants me to have one more load hauled for him when that is done we will settle up. I send a little piece from the "Star"[164] all that sheet does is to abuse the President and glorify Gov Brown and now like some other papers in the country it is indulging its spite and venom in abusing the Congress. do you not think it would have been better to let Gov Foote keep on when he started to Washington?

The children make a dreadful fuss around me as I write, and it is hard to write when they are all here in one little room. I believe I have written you all I can think of for the present perhaps I will add more tonight.

I wish you could see Susie, she is very lively and laughs so much Eliza and I call her "Mrs. Shepherd" She has cried a great deal to-day but whenever she quits crying she goes to [laughing] [?]

I will send this letter to Lexington tomorrow, that will make it leave one day sooner than if I mailed it here. I will write again by Tuesdays mail. I suppose I will certainly get more letters from you next Friday You write that you have been sick. I hope you are entirely recovered now. I can but feel very anxious about you, Dear

164. The reference must be to the *Star of the South* published in Elberton, Georgia, beginning in 1859, out of which grew the Elberton *Star*, established in 1880. See Rabun L. Brantley, *Georgia Journalism of the Civil War Period* (Nashville, 1929), 36.

Love. Suppose you were to get sick, oh, what would I do. I should be wretched about you and fear all the time that you needed my nursing and attention and I do not know how I could get to you. I would have to wean the baby to go and leave her at home, but I hope such trouble is not in store for us. Do take care of yourself, and if your health fails do come home immediately. but do not expose yourself in inclement weather to come home. Ah me, you dont know how anxious I am to see you, to have you at home again. When do you think you can come?

Ever my dearest, Your devoted wife
Mary F. Akin

Elberton Jan 29th 1865

MY DEAR HUSBAND, I received your letters of the 14th & 17th last Friday and I felt much relieved to know you were well when you wrote. You dont know my dear how bad I feel when I know you have your socks to me[nd]. I reproach myself for not having had more knit for you to take with you and I am sorry I did[n't] run thread all over the heels & toes of those you have it would have made them last so much longer, and I expect your flanel drawers are wearing out too. can you not hire some one to mend your drawers when they need it. I do not think dear husband you ought to deny yourself the comfort of having your clothes washed as often as you did at home *especially your handkerchiefs* In one letter you say you use them until they are so soiled you are ashamed of them. I dont think that is right. You ought always to have clean handkerchiefs, it is such a comfort and what ever will make you comfortable while away from home you ought to have. Does not washing your head so often make your hair look very dry and stiff. I should think it would. I am sorry to know you dont sleep well at night. You ask me to correct you if you spell wrong, in telling me of your sleeplessness you say you "rool over & over" I know you know how to spell "roll" but was not noticing when you wrote to me how you were spelling.

Your long continued absence from home is most trying to me. I dont know how I could love you any better than I do now, but I suppose I will enjoy your presence at home more after so long a separation than I can have before as to getting *used* to your being away I dont think I ever could, even if I knew we could meet no more on earth I think then all my thoughts of you would be of when you should meet hereafter, and I should never under *any circumstances* cease to miss and your constant and kind care and thoughtfulness of me and of our children. You write as you have often talked to me about what you feel or think about my marrying again if you should ever die. My dear husband it is very painful to me for you to talk about such things, more painful for you to write about it. dont do so any more. None of us can *know* what we will do in the future, but if I know my own heart I would never do such a thing, and oh, if I should be so dreadfully unfortunate as to be a widow may the Lord deliver me from the folly, and in my case it would be the wickedness, of ever marrying again. If you love me and I believe you do, never say anything more to me on this subject. And you write of how free from all earthly care of every kind you would have me to live if you could, Do you know I dont want to live that way. I prefer some hardships, adversity and afflictions to a life of entire ease, freedom from care & sorrow. If I never had any sorrows, cares, and *hardships* to bear I should fear the Lord had forgotten me, and was allowing me all my good in this "present life." and such a life of ease was never intended for any of God's children. No, I want to bear my share of the burden of life and I pray God I may be enabled to bear it cheerfully & patiently to the end.

In your letter of the 17th you tell me of how few letters you get from me. I fear you never will get all I have written you. I write you twice some times three times every week. I *never* fail to write to you twice a week anyhow. I wrote to you of the result of my asking Mr. Wall & Mr. Tate to take interest-bearing treasury notes in payment of what you owed them. I have written to Mr. Mattox and have no doubt his answer will be the same as the others, for I know through Col Rochester that he has many of those notes, sent them to Augusta by Col Rochester to be sold, but Col R would not sell them because he could get but 40 cts in the dollar for them. Col Rochester called to see me last friday about dinner time. I had sent him word by Mrs. Haire that I wished to get some spool thread from him. he brought it to me. I had finished my dinner when he got here, but I soon had the back bone that was left warmed over a few nice biscuit made and some half & half coffee and I think he enjoyed his dinner. Spool thread is selling here at 10 & 12 dollars a spool. I got three spools of thread and a good sized hank of flax from Col Rochester for $20.00 I believe I told you that needles sold here at from 10 to 20 dollars a paper. Col Rochester is well acquainted with Mrs. Tubman[165] of Augusta who was allowed by the Federal authorities to spend last

165. Mrs. Emily H. Tubman was an affluent and philanthropic resident of Augusta. As a child in Kentucky she had been a ward of Henry Clay. Tubman High School for girls and the Tubman Home for aged women, in Augusta, both are named for her. Information provided by Florence Fleming (Mrs. James) Corley, of Marietta, Ga., whose M. A. thesis at Emory University (1955) was "Augusta, Georgia, A Confederate City."

summer in Kentucky. She gave Col R many interesting particulars of Federal rule in Kentucky. She ascertained without the least doubt that there is a prison *full* of southern women in Louisville and they are most strictly guarded and allowed no communication with their friends. All are afraid to speak their sentiments even to their nearest friends, and such I fear will be our fate in Ga before many months. Col R says he is astonished at the extent of dysloyal sentiment in Augusta. He has two sons in prison have been in a long time and he is so hopeful of their early exchange that he bought or tried to buy some jeans at Vails the other day to make them some pants. he boards at Mr. Burton's near Mr. Haire's. I wrote you that I intended letting Mr. Perry Bruce have the wagon to go over to Lexington. Bob carried him and his wife & a lot of things she expected to take to Augusta to sell to Lexington last Friday and came back Saturday. Miss Mason came back in the wagon with Bob and when he got to Mr. Haire's, Mrs. Upshaw & Alice Latimer got in the wagon and came on to see us, got here a little after dark. I do not know how long they will stay. They tell me Robert Latimer and his wife are expected in Ga very soon Robert L's command has been ordered to Carolina and he wishes to buy a place in Ga or Ala and wishes his mother and wife to live together. Mrs. Latimer is still [at the] Haire's and has no prospect of getting away from there any time soon. Mr. Haire starts next Monday up to Bartow county with the faint hope of finding something there belonging to him and trying to save it. We hear that Col Price is sorry he went back. he has very little to live on and no prospect of buying provisions until another crop is made. Mr. Gilreath is having as his daughter Betty says "scratching" times to get along, recently he has had to go for Craven's family and bring them over here to live with them, and now Jabez's family, a wife and nine children, have all come to this county and are very dependent on the old man for a living. He speaks of taking his family back to Bortow in March and trying to make a corn crop there.

This morning Verdy had wet her drawers and even her stocking I shamed her very much for it, told he she was a very dirty girl asked her if she were not ashamed. she looked very sad and answered "Yes Mam I am ashamed" and then with the most humble contrite expression I ever saw added "Whip me mother I wont cry one bit." I liked to have cried myself when she said that to me. She will not get up in the morning until she has hugged & kissed Eliza and [got] her permission to get up. her hands and wrists are so chapped with the cold they are much swollen and so painful she cried about them and

Katie's are almost as bad as Verdy's and Johnnys hands look dreadfully. Have we not had very cold weather for the last week, most of the time I've been suffering with diarrhea and I dont think I ever suffered more with the cold, and I could not sleep warm altho' I had a great deal of cover on my bed, and wd [would] sleep in my sack. Now if you had been here I would not have suffered so much with cold at night. Well dear, I have written part of this letter while they were all talking around me and making all sorts of a noise and now it is near 10 oclock and all have gone to bed but Lotty and I and I am getting tired I will have to stop and finish tomorrow night. I had forgotten to tell you I went over to see Mrs. Dobbs Saturday evening. her father died recently and her mother intended selling out all she had tomorrow and is coming here for the present, she is afraid to stay so near the enemy, and young David Dobbs has gone to be at the sale and assist her in moving over to Ga. he left here last Thursday & it is uncertain when he will return. Mrs. Dobbs is still going about, and looks very well. I have received the money you sent by Capt. Scott. Mr. Little sent it to me by Bob. I was very glad to get it. I will write more tomorrow night Good night my dear dear husband.

Tuesday morning Jan. 30th) Yesterday morning, Mrs. Upshaw and I went to see Mrs. J. H. Jones, Mrs. U–to return Mrs J–call and I went with her Mrs. Jones you know has been to see me twice and I therefore felt no hesitancy in calling again. While there Mrs Jones & I got to talking of the state of the country she tells me that there are a great many men in this county and even in this place who are anxious for reconstruction, anxious for Ga to go back in the U. S. She told me she had heard that it was reported the wife of one of the representatives from Ga, and she told her name, had said her husband had written to her to have no fears peace would be made *very soon* and many persons were much rejoiced to hear it they seemed to think what Mrs. E– said must certainly be so, and of great importance.[166] I was in Mr. Vail's store just before I went up to Major Jones' and several gentlemen asked very eagerly, I thought [remainder of letter missing.]

Elberton Feb 1st 1865

MY DEAR HUSBAND Yesterday I received three letters from you, of the 17th & 18th, one of the 20th, & one of the 23rd. Your long affectionate and kind letters are very cheering to me. I feel almost crazy to see you sometimes, and how slowly the time passes. I read & reread the papers hoping I will see something there about the adjournment

166. Mrs. E. must have been the wife of Joseph H. Echols as he was the only Georgia Congressman at this time whose name began with an "E."

of Congress but I see nothing encouraging and fear it will be April before you get home. Oh, what a long weary time it will be. This morning I heard Cousin Betsy Blackwell was in town. I went to Dr. Jones' to see her and spent several hours there. While there Col Boman came in, he asked about the news you wrote, what you said about peace etc. I read to him what you had written, he talked as if it were a fixed fact that we were to have peace so soon it was unnecessary to make any effort to meet Sherman's advancing army, or to respond in any way to Gen Lee's call for subsistence for his army. he also seemed to be certain that England and France had been dictating to Lincoln the terms of peace and he talked as if he rather favored *reconstruction.* said he much preferred reconstruction to an alliance with any of the European powers, he evidently dont hate a yankee as I do. I thought Col Boman a very pleasant man and he enquired most kindly after your welfare. Every one here seems to take it for granted or a certainty that we will very soon have peace. I certainly hope it, but with all the lights before me that I now have I can not see that it is a certain thing. This evening I went to see Mrs. Dobbs for a little while she was very unwell. I wrote you her husband had gone to Carolina. She has made all her arrangements about getting some old lady as well as the Doctor to stay with her when she needs them and I have urged her to call on me for any assistance she may need. old man Dobbs was not at home. Mrs. D- told me how much trouble his grand daughters were to him and how lost he was to know what to do with them. As I came home I "met up" with Cousin Sally and Miss Lucy Vail and they came home with me and sat awhile. Cousin Sally says she has been looking for that letter from you. Mrs. Upshaw went home Tuesday evening Mr. Burton came in town in his buggy and offered to take her home. she did not know when she would have another opportunity of going and therefore went with him. Alice is still with us. Mr. George Gilreath took dinner here tuesday. he tells me there is much suffering among the people of Bartow county for want of food. he also told me that Thomas' army was at Rome. I see nothing in the papers to make me think that is so but if it is the people in that county must be suffering greatly, the negros that have been carried back there will all leave. I heard that Lewis Tumlin[167] had carried his negros to Bartow to make a crop and now had gone there to take them away because he could not get food

167. Lewis Tumlin was a self-made man who in the antebellum period became one of Cass County's most affluent residents. He owned much land and other property, including numerous slaves. He was active in politics and was a presidential elector for Breckinridge and Lane in 1860. For a sketch of Tumlin, see Cunyus, *History of Bartow County*, 97-98.

for them up there. We also hear that Hoods army is being sent to Augusta

Thursday Feb 2nd—Having heard that I could get oats at a very reasonable price from a Mr. Snelling in the flat woods I sent Bob and Elbert there yesterday to get some. All the oats he had was engaged but Elbert bought three large loads of oats straw & a good deal of chaff with it for $25.00. I got the three loads for 25.00 I have not yet been able to get any shucks. Mr. Wall has promised me two loads after awhile. Bob brought one load of straw yesterday and has gone for another to-day will go again to-morrow then I will make him haul the fodder from Mr. Cleveland's. Bob is more idle and careless than I have ever known him to be, or it seems to me he is, he always seems to be doing something but gets nothing done, he feeds the mules night and morning and that is about all he does. Allen cuts all the wood and does many other things that it is really Bob's business to attend to. You must excuse my telling you anything of this kind that will disturb you, but I do have so many little things to vex and annoy me I can not help speaking out sometimes about it, and then the children require so much attention I feel almost crazy sometimes waiting on them. Little Susie is getting to be a real good little baby. I send her to Rachel's house at night and on ironing days. I never saw a baby love to laugh and to be kissed as she does. Katie is very fat and more healthy now than any child we have. Elbert has a very sore eye, it is much swollen and inflamed. Warren is not very well complains some times of a pain in his side. I would not be surprised if he was subject to attacks of pneumonia every spring, he is so careless he never knows how to take care of himself. Johnny is very thin and sallow, he is sometimes so much opposed to learning his book I let him alone for a few days, then by persuasions and some few threats of punishment I get him to begin again.

I am surprised to hear of Mr. Saxon's movements about leaving the country. do you think he will really go, and how does he expect to support his family if he does go? In your letter of the 20th you ask if Pa or Ma has ever written me about sending Liz back they have not, *if they had I would certainly have mentioned it to you.* I have received but one letter from Ma since you went away. I told you all she said in that that would interest you. I received one from Sue soon after you left home those are the only letters I have received from any of them. I have received a few short notes from brother William a few letters from Aunty and they are all I have received except one from Mrs. Land. I keep all your letters the envelopes are scarcely worth turning they are so damaged & soiled when they get here, and so full I often split them in getting your letters out of them. You must be sure to keep all the envelopes of the letters you receive while in Richmond and when you come home I will turn them all for our own use. I do not often write to you three times a week. I really do not have the time. You know I write very slowly and then having so many little household affairs to attend to and serving to do too. I am kept very busy, indeed from early in the morning until nine oclock every night, and when nine oclock comes I am so tired I get nervous and restless and can not write because I can not sit still, then I have to go to bed am sleeping and waking up taking short naps all night. I generally get up as soon as it is light. I do not keep an account of all I spend. I have heard nothing from Mr. Cobb. I wish he would bring or send the money so I could pay what you owe, would 1,500 dollars pay for it all. If you go to Bartow in the Spring Elbert and Warren will be very anxious to go with you. I expect you will have to go in your wagon. Sam Patton is dead, was wounded in Sept carried to a hospital in Macon where he lingered until some time in December, then died a happy Christian, his obituary is in the last Atlanta Intelligencer. he was 42 years old, I had no idea he was that old. Is Mrs. Frank Jackson's husband a prisoner? I hear some *dreadful* reports about Dr. Rambant's daughter . . . [MS torn-] The servants tell me Mrs. Dobbs has a little daughter born this morning I am going to send round after dinner to know if it is so, and ask how she is. I must stop writing now and go to doubling some stocking thread.

Friday morning Feb 3rd Well, I sent to Mrs. Dobbs yesterday to know how she was. she has a little daughter born yesterday morning and was doing very well. I intended going round there to-day, but the rain is falling so fast I can not go. I will send Rachel again some time to-day to find out how she is getting on and know if she needs any thing. I have let her have a small matress for her children and I think she will let me know if she needs anything. She expects Mr. Dobbs home to-morrow and I hope he will come the old man is already wretched because he cannot hear from him. Yesterday morning Mrs. J. H. Jones and her two daughters called to see us they thought Mrs. Upshaw was with us there call was very formal they only staid about ten or fifteen minutes. Katie went in the parlor and spoke to the ladies and kissed them. Verdy always goes in the parlor when I have

[remainder of letter missing]

☆ 9 ☆

"God Holds the Curtain of the Future"

Richmond, Va.
Decr 15th 1864

MY DEAR SON [ELBERT]: Having eight letters on my table unanswered, besides much labour to preform, I have not a great deal of time to spend in answering your very welcome letter of the 3rd inst.

I am much pleased to see so much more thought exhibited in your last letter than any previous one I have received from you. It furnishes evidence of improvement in the right direction. One must *think* if he ever succeeds in *any* thing. You should not only think, but think before you *act*. Decide *what* you want to do, examine well all the pros and cons, *think* about it, – not only of the present results, but how it will work or operate in the future – and then, when well satisfied that it is *right*, carry it out. (Senator Hill has called to see me, I had to stop writing, he has just left, it is now after eight oclock at night and I can not write much to you.)

You should not only *think* before acting, but you should have *decision* and *firmness* in your purpose. To be of one opinion to-day and another to-morrow – set out in the pursuit of one object, and immediately change about and start after another – will show a want of *firmness* in your purpose, a fickleness in your pursuits, & will soon destroy all confindence in yourself, while no one else can rely upon you. If you will think and reason well *before* acting, changing about will [not] often be necessary. But when convinced you are in error, it will not only not be wrong to acknowledge it, but highly commendable, praiseworthy, magnanimous and right to do so; and if any injury has been done by your errors at once repair it if in your power. I am glad to see that you now think it was well you did not purchase a gun. I told you it would be, at present prices of powder and shot a constant heavy expense, if you used it much. It is not wise to spend all of one's hard earnings in mere pleasure. Better keep it, and make it help you, and by and by when unable to work you may have something to live on in ease and comfort. *Money at interest* is *always*

Editor's Note: The letters in this chapter were found among the personal effects of the late Paul F. Akin, too late for inclusion at the proper place in the chronological sequence.

making something – day and night it is increasing – whether you are asleep or awake it is accumulating. But once spent it is gone forever, if spent for mere pleasure or present enjoyment. Count the interest on five hundred dollars at seven per cent per annum for twenty years, compounding it yearly and write me the amount the whole sum will be. You will see that it will be greatly increased. In spending money, as a general rule, you should not look to present pleasure or enjoyment, but to future, permanent good. It is very essential to standing in this world that you should have enough of this world's goods to support and take care of yourself, to make you independent. And to have this you will have to labour and toil, and *save* what you make unless you are more fortunate than I've been.

Having spoken yesterday and to-day on a very important question (a bill pending before the House to compel those who have left the country to avoid military service to return or sequestrate their property for the use of minor children of deceased soldiers), I feel tired, and to supply my lack of advice, I enclose you a letter from Genl Lee to one of his sons, written in 1852, and request you and your brother to read it, and to ask your mother to past[e] it in her scrap book where you can often read it and memorise it. I wish you to examine the manner the doors and windows to the crib and stable are hung and if you think they are not safe that they do not protect my mules and corn from rogues, you must have iron hinges made and put on. The loss of two bushels [of] corn will be greater than the cost of the hinges. See that the windows can not be opened from the out side. I have seen wood hinges that were strong and good. The hinges to my father's cribs were made of wood. But those to the crib and stables on the lot you are on may be worthless. How are they made and fastened on?

I handed you two dollars to pay ferriage and then gave you ten dollars for you and Warren, and expected if you bought the plank that your mother would pay for it, and you and Warren still have five dollars each.

You say "the stable and corncrib is finished." Is that correct?

Did you haul 560 bushles [of] fodder from Judge Herndon's at one load? Surely not. Weigh twenty five bundles and see what they weigh, and keep a memorandum of the weight. Take the bundles as you come to them, so that they will be a fair average of the whole. Write me a long letter and take pains in writing, spelling and grammar.

Kiss your mother and all your brothers and sisters for me.

Your fondly devoted father
Warren Akin

[P. S.] I wrote to your mother yesterday and sent it by *hand to day*.

Richmond, Va.
Decr 31st 1864.

MY DEAR SWEET DARLING: This is the last day of the year. In a few hours 1864 will be gone forever, and I am writing to my sweet wife for the last time in this year. Look back for twelve brief months and behold the wonderful changes that have taken place. A year ago we were at our comfortable home, where we have lived so many years. We had many comforts about us. Our friends were around us, the colleges and our little town standing. Now our house is in ashes, colleges and town burnt, our friends scattered, we are far from our homes and one more child to provide for, while our means are greatly curtailed and every day are becoming less. A year ago and many hoped and believed the war would be at an end before this, and our warworn soldiers all at home in peace. But there is no prospect of peace, but a reasonable probability of four years more of war. And what may be our condition at the end of four years to come, if we are alive? But God holds the curtain of the future, and he alone can draw it aside to enable us to behold the fate that awaits us. Let us not therefore trouble ourselves about it, so far as this world is concerned; but try to be patient and resigned – endeavouring to feel that we are in His hands, that He will take care of us, and that He doeth all things well. The year now closing, has had in it many trials and troubles – our losses have been great, our fare coarse and scanty, compared with former years, but viewing the whole ground, considering all the circumstances, and remembering how much more fortunate and blessed we have been than thousands of others, have we not much cause for thankfulness and gratitude to God for his goodness, mercy and lovingkindness towards us? None of our loved ones have been taken from us. When you the children and our house were in the power of the enemies they treated you all much better than many others. I have been kept out of their hands. And when two of our children were *very* sick. God raised them up again. Has He not been very good to us? "Surely goodness and mercy have followed me all the days of my life." Suppose the Yankees had captured me and carried me off to a northern prison? I might now have been dead, or where you could not hear from me, suffering from cold, hunger or disease. How terrible would have been your condition, as well as mine. And suppose our dear children, Warren and Mary, had died. How would we have borne it? Thank the Lord for all his mercies towards us! O for a heart more thankful, humble, patient and resigned! Let us try to be thankful and cheerful, and "having food and raiment to be therewith content."

I am sorry to hear that the older children are so dissatisfied with their condition. When Warren & Elbert are in the army, having half enough to eat, suffering with cold and marching in the rain; and when Eliza is in some cabin cooking her food and having but little to cook, and washing her own clothes and not having much to wash, they will look back to *the good days they spent in Elberton.* If they *knew* how many there are who are suffering for the most common necessaries of life – for bread, clothing, shoes and shelter, they would not think their lot a hard one. They would thank God, as they ought, that they are so comfortably situated. Hundreds about this town are almost starving. I have seen them trying to sell a few old books to get something to live on, and in the street picking up little pieces of coal and chips, that had been swept out, to make a little fire. Hundreds in this city, and all over the country will lie down hungry to-night and sleep cold and get up to-morrow hungry and cold. Let my children remember these things, and thank God and be happy that they are so comfortably situated. If I *knew,* to-night, that they would never be in any worse condition, how happy I would be. I would close this year feeling happier than at any time passing through it. But we should not be distressed because our children act unwisely, and fret themselves unnecessarily. Children, will be children, and we can not make old folks of them. Indeed, we should not if we could. I know that, when I was a boy, I did many foolish things, and our children will learn, after a while, that they too, have acted foolishly. Experience is the only teacher for many persons, and they may be taught by it after a while. How are Eliza, Elbert and Warren engaged? Keep them *employed* at something. *Make* the boys study their books. *Make* them sit down in your room and study. Keep them engaged at something *every day*, and they will not have time to be dissatisfied. They will sleep at night and enjoy relaxation from study and labour. They *must* study. I will have to see how much they have learned when I get home. *I mean exactly what I say*. I have written to you several times that Bro. Gilreath promised to hire out Floyd and Charles for me, and I suppose he has done so, but if he should not do so, I requested you to request Major Jones to do so for me. Has Bro. Gilreath gone back to Bartow? I wrote him some weeks since to write me how to send him some money if I collected it for him. I have since collected the money and wrote him immediately, but do not hear from him. Please write him a note that I have collected his money and wish him to write me *how* and to what place I must send him his money. I will now cease writing for *this year*, as I have some work to do before sleeping. It has been snowing here all day, but melting and the sidwalks & crossings are very sloppy. The year closes with the earth mantled in white, a happy omen I hope.

1865. January 1st –

The *last* word written in the year 1864 by me was to my very dear, sweet, wife, and the *first* written in the year 1865 is also to my darling. Do you love me dearest like you used to? Do you love me as well as you did on the 12th day of October, 1848? Will you always love me? If I should live to be old, infirm and helpless, will my darling still love me, nurse me and care for me, as she has done heretofore? Will you still sit by me and hold my hand and try to soothe me to sleep and watch me while sleeping? Will you have for me that same fond tenderness and affection you have always exhibited and felt for me, through so many years of trouble and trial? When the brightness of the eye, the elasticity of step, vigour of mind and strength of body are all gone will my dear darling wife still love me fondly; still administer, with tenderest affection, to all my necessities, anticipate all my wants and feel and manifest for me the same devotion she has always done! Will she sit by me when dying, close my eyes in death and love me when I'm cold in the grave? Yes, yes, I know from the past she will do all this and far more than words can express. And yet, why do I ask such questions? I know not. And yet I love thus to write you. My heart's fondest, tenderest affection runs out after you, it seems to me, more ardently, with more pure devotion, with more intensity of feeling than at any time in all my life. It seems that I love you as I never loved you before. It is impossible for me to describe my feelings. My desire to be with you, to talk to you, to embrace you far surpasses any thing I ever felt before. Eternity alone, my darling, will reveal my heart's fond love and pure devotion for you. O, my dear sweet cherub, *you* know not and *I* can not tell you how much I love you. O for one hour to behold thy beautiful face, thy sweet smile and to hear thy loved voice. But ah! loved one, I may not see you for months to come. How can I bear the long absence? How shall I pass the long, long weeks and months? Do write me some sweet, cheering words of comfort and hope. Do tell me of your heart's fond love, write sweet loving words, that will fall on my heart more soft and soothing, more delightful and enrapturing, than sweetest strains of melody when awaking from a dreaming visit to angelic abodes. Let thy tender and affectionate words fall on my anxious heart with an effect similar to that produced on the troubled sea, when the waters heard the Saviour saying "peace be still." And though my heart is anxious and troubled, it is not a painful anxiety, a troubled spirit – I am anxious to see you and my dear children. Anxious to hear the soft melody of music coming from lips, moved by hearts that love me. Here springs my anxiety. And will you not give me a long sweet letter? Do my dear darling write me one of your sweetest letters in reply to this. Let it be one full of tenderness and love, making the "old time come oer me." Write me all the little sweet sayings of my dear children. Send me a "bundle of love," filled with soft, sweet tender words, and kiss them all many times for me. Well my darling, this is sunday night, and I will lay me down to sleep. Good night sweetest one, good night.

"All angels bless and guard thee."

Your devoted husband
Warren Akin

Monday morning, Jany 2nd. No letter from you this morning my precious. The weather is very cold. Ice on all the side walks. The snow melted a little yesterday, and every thing is frozen up this morning. Well, guess who slept with me last night? I venture you would not guess in a week. Genl Wofford came to my room, and asked to board a few days, and I took him in my room & shared my bed with him. There was no other way for him to stay. A strange room mate & bed fellow for *me*. And I cant sleep much. His presence prevented me from writing as much to you as I desired and intended. My "new year's gift," darling, therefore, much shorter than I wished. But you will, I hope take the will for the deed. Do write me a little, dearest, *every day*. I do not expect to write you so much this week as the last one, but hope you will receive two letters every mail. Do make my children, darling, feel how much I love them, and get them to write me often. Kiss all for me. May God bless you all.

Warren

House of Representatives,
Richmond, Va.
Jany. 17th 1865

MY DEAR WIFE: I came early to the Hall of the House hoping to hear from you, but the mail is not distributed and I commence to write you a few lines on Cap paper. I have no news to write. I mailed a letter to you yesterday. One to Judge Land, also.

Well the mail is opened and I again receive no letter from you. How long, O how long shall I be in suspense, and fail to hear from my darling? I know you can have no adequate idea of my desire to hear from you. The entire satisfaction I have that the failure to receive letters is from no fault of yours, is some comfort. At least, it prevents my becoming wretched. Only think that your letters of the 30th ult. and 6th inst. have not yet been received. One 18 days and the the other eleven days out. Well neither you nor I can avoid it, and I will *try* to be resigned to my fate, and be as patient as possible. I am *hoping on* every day, and trust my hopes will be realized the next day, and trust they will to-morrow.

I know not what to write you. I went last night, in the parlor at my boarding house. There were a young married lady, a young widow and a young lady, but I could not get any one to play on the piano. The young widow is a good looking lady. Her husband has been dead four years, she is still in black. Indeed the most of the women are still in black and the whole land is mourning and grief is felt in every family.

Humphrey Marshall of Ky. is making a most eloquent speech, and is frequently cheered on the floor and in the gallery. I hope his remarks will be published & that you will see them in the Sentinel. I must close for this time.

God bless you dearest and my dear children. Kiss them all for me. Love to Cousin Sally.

Your loving & devoted husband
Warren Akin

☆ ☆ ☆

Index